The New Music Industry

Adapting, Growing, and Thriving in The Information Age

By: David Andrew Wiebe (www.DAWCast.com)
Cover Design By: David Andrew Wiebe
Cover & Author Photography By: Greg Parke

Table Of Contents

Create an Unforgettable Live Experience / Conclusion / What I Like / What I Don't Like / Action Steps

8. Radio

Introduction to Radio / DJs are Expert Marketers / The Different Types of Radio / Radio Campaigns / My Experience / How to Promote Your Music with Radio / Conclusion / What I Like / What I Don't Like / Action Steps

9. Music Instruction

Introduction to Music Instruction / The Different Types of Music Instruction / Wages / Turnover / Attitude / 10 Essential Characteristics of Successful Music Instructors / Conclusion / What I Like / What I Don't Like / Action Steps

10. Copywriting

Introduction to Copywriting / Spelling & Grammar / Band or Artist Bio / Press Releases / 13 Ways to Become a Better Copywriter / Conclusion / What I Like / What I Don't Like / Action Steps

11. Blogging

Introduction to Blogging / Create a Blogging Schedule / Have a Content (Marketing) Strategy) / Content Marketing Trifecta / Schedule Posts / Why Blog? / Comments / 9 Things to Blog About as a Musician / Conclusion / What I Like / What I Don't Like / Action Steps

12. Podcasting

Introduction to Podcasting / Target Market / Goals / Getting Started /
Hosting / Format / How to Promote Your Podcast and Expand Your
Audience / Conclusion / What I Like / What I Don't Like / Action Steps

Introduction to Email Marketing / Marketing Messages / Email
Marketing Tools / Tour by Email / Email Signature / Email Address /
Etiquette / 12 Effective Email Marketing Strategies / Conclusion /
What I Like / What I Don't Like / Action Steps

Introduction to Social Media / Keep Informed / Frequent Engagement
/ Third Party Tools / Facebook / Twitter / LinkedIn / Pinterest /
Google+ / Tumblr / Instagram / MySpace / Bandcamp & Music
Distribution / How to Develop a Successful Social Media Strategy /
Conclusion / What I Like / What I Don't Like / Action Steps

Introduction to YouTube & Video Marketing / OneLoad / The
Importance of Your Video's Title / How to Optimize Your Video's
Description / Populate Your Profile / Interact / Iterate / Stay
Consistent / How to be Successful on YouTube / Conclusion / What I
Like / What I Don't Like / Action Steps

1. Foreword

The independent music landscape is one of the most challenging of any profession. The rules are arbitrary and easily broken. Vultures abound, and they'll be there if you're not aware of your position at all times. Also, the competition is far beyond fierce. It's legitimately overpopulated.

In order to approach the music industry properly, we need to first examine why we're in it in the first place. Sales are the wrong reason. Music is the right reason. Then, we must remove any defined plan or definition of the way things are, as that will limit our efforts and true creativity. Life is much wider than our strategies. Expectations are best dropped. Most importantly, discard "mountain view" thinking.

Artists are often guilty of wanting to go from point A to point Z, and advertisers know this. Promotion companies know this. Record labels and licensing companies know this. And you can bet some of them take advantage. It's the Idol syndrome. We all want to jump from the couch to the television screen, but there's no realism in that story. Are you ready to walk your path step by step? If so, you'll need to fill in every blank, act on every detail, to send emails, to ship packages, to post statuses, to play dingy bars, to reach out to professionals, to save money and invest in yourself.

Once we're clear of "mountain view" thinking, we're ready to act, and one thing that is the most helpful is honest communication. David Andrew Wiebe provides just that, both through his website and this book. There is no pretension or abstraction at work here, and the reader is better off for it. He draws on his 12 years of self-promotion experience and is refreshingly open about his limitations and follies, a style I myself think is among the best ways to teach. Through negation, we find our path. From the basics of blogging, bio writing, social media, and podcasting to music video promotion, David covers a wide range of steps to help you start scaling your individual mountain.

I hope this book enriches your musical path.

James Moore, CEO of Independent Music Promotions & author of "Your Band Is A Virus"

To check out James' website and book, go to:
http://dawcast.com/the-new-music-industry-resource-list/

2. Introduction

I started working on this project in the fall of 2012.

I had already begun working on an book project prior to that, but I ended up scrapping it because I didn't think any musician would want to read the complete encyclopaedia on personal success and self-development. Instead of keeping my focus on matters pertaining to music and what I knew best, I somehow ended up branching off into many unrelated topics.

When I made the decision to start from scratch in 2012, I had just sold my house. I was able to pay off all of my debts and bless my mom too. This allowed me to begin this project from a place of clear-headedness and financial security. The vision for the book started to form rather rapidly after that.

Though I didn't know this at first, I now know that what I have been working on is **the guide I wish I had when I was first getting started in music**. With over 13 years of experience behind me, it's taken a lot of trial and error to get to where I'm at.

There are many great resources out there today, but when I was first beginning to take interest in building a music career in the early 2000s, there still wasn't that much reliable information available. From the basics of music distribution to radio promotion, there were a lot of important things I was entirely clueless about.

Not to mention the fact that the industry was going through a lot of change, and it *still* is.

But I'm glad that I went through what I did, because I now have the opportunity to pass on my experiences and knowledge to help others achieve their musical dreams.

I don't pretend to know everything. However, if you read this book with an open mind, I believe you'll be able to forego the many years of trial and error I had to endure. Your starting point should look remarkably different from mine if you apply what you learn. I hope you do.

Congratulations, friend. You are in the right place at the right time. The fact that you purchased this material shows that you are a cut above average. It shows that you want to learn and grow and become better than you are today, and that's what's required of you in order to see your dreams become a reality.

3. The New Music Industry

We are currently seeing one of the biggest shifts the music industry has ever known. One of the primary components of this mass movement is the *format shift*. As advisor, author and blogger Andrew Dubber has it, the revenue and distribution model for musicians has changed from patronage (way back in the days of Bach; pun intended), to live performance, to print publishing, to recording, to radio and synchronization. **We are witnesses to a shift of a similar nature**, only on a much larger scale.

Here is a brief overview:

The Compact Disc is showing some signs of hanging on, but it seems clear that it's not going to remain a mainstay. At the very least, it's no longer the primary means of music consumption. Digital downloads were initially thought to be the obvious replacement, yet they are somewhat stagnant and haven't fully overtaken CD sales. Meanwhile, vinyl sales have been seeing a peculiar but steady rise since 2004. By Dubber's account, it's just a blip on the radar and not to be taken as a full-fledged trend. *Yet*. Streaming sites are gaining in popularity, controversy along with them.

Plainly, the industry is changing and adapting in other ways as well. I actually wrote about this new paradigm on the TuneCity blog in December 2012, but since it can't be found online anymore, I'm going to summarize the key points here for your benefit:

1) Artists need to be conscious about adding more value to their fans and people in general. This doesn't mean that music has no value; rather, the artists who are consistently offering more and are actively engaging with their fans are the ones growing their fan base. People care more about *experience* than the music itself. Being more transparent and accessible is one of many ways artists are building larger communities of followers. **Engagement** is a key component.

2) **Campaigns** are the name of the game, and I'm not just talking crowdfunding campaigns either (although that is definitely relevant). Social media contests, giveaways, limited free releases, surveys and a variety of other one-offs and concerted promotional efforts are helping artists get the attention of the media and new fans (but it all starts with the existing fan base).

3) As an artist, it's important to build a **community** (or multiple communities) of likeminded people who share similar ideas and interests. People today seem to embrace their niche likes and dislikes more openly and readily than ever before. When Baby Boomers got going in a particular direction, it was *mass movement*, as their adoption of mainstream media and music was almost universal. They also had less *choice*. Today, people have more choice and are much harder to pin down, with Techno fans listening to Country, and Windows users using Apple devices.

4) **Collaboration**, piggybacking, trend-reading, whatever you want to call it… these are some of the ways artists are building their fan base today, usually using the video medium. Artists like Pomplamoose, Lindsey Stirling, Igor Presnyakov, OK Go, Walk off the Earth and Tiffany Alvord are all examples of artists that are appealing to a novelty sense, doing something unique or unusual, or reinterpreting popular songs. This medium seems to be working out pretty well for them.

5) **Vinyl** is a growth market sector, as already noted. I believe it's shaping up to be more than just a passing trend. There are two things every artist should address if they are interested in putting their music on a vinyl record: 1) the quality of their music (i.e. does it have dynamics?), and 2) the cohesiveness of the entire album (i.e. vinyl records are generally listened to all the way through).

6) **Social media** is a really big deal. Facebook has over 1.4 billion users, and Google+ has over 540 million. I don't know how you could create a profitable music career today without using social media (although I'm sure there is a way), so that should at least hint at its importance.

7) As already noted, most artists listed in point 4 are using video and **YouTube** as a vital part of their online strategy. **Video marketing** is massive, and it's opening up a variety of opportunities for artists. According to

Huffington Post, YouTube has over one billion active users on a monthly basis.

8) This may come as a surprise to some, but getting on the **radio** still appears to be one of the best ways to get immediate and widespread exposure for artists. DJs come from a long tradition of being tastemakers; plugging and promoting things they enjoy. Often music.

9) Although the **touring** scene has changed considerably, for artists seeking label support, it's absolutely necessary to be touring on a regular basis (work ethic is of great importance to A&R reps). Live performance isn't always lucrative for indie artists, but in most cases it's still necessary. Believe it or not, some little known bands (popular but not household names) make six-figure incomes on touring alone.

10) Many opportunities are opening up in the **music licensing and placement** department thanks to the influx of TV shows, commercials, movies, video games and other entertainment mediums. With that in mind, reading a couple of Helen Austin's articles should prompt one to realize that it isn't something you fall in to by accident. It takes great focus and dedication, and it's a sector with considerable competition as well. The demand for placements is going up, competition along with it.

11) **Streaming sites** are also a huge component of the new music industry, and I anticipate many changes taking place in this sector in years to come. Some of the metrics and infographics that have come out depicting the income potential from music streaming are a little disheartening to be blunt. However, the reality of it seems to be that a single stream actually pays more than your average spin on the radio. It's simply a difference in numbers; airplay on the radio reaches many people, while a single stream only reaches one person. Even if streaming can't be counted on for your living expenses, it can be an additional income source, and having multiple income sources is helpful if not obligatory for career-minded independent artists today.

For an industry that was essentially only concerned with recording, radio, touring, distribution and retail sales throughout the 80s and 90s, the aforementioned list may seem a little overwhelming. However, I would encourage you to keep this list in the back of your mind as you read the remainder of this book.

>> Tools & Tips

To access these and other resources, go to:
http://dawcast.com/the-new-music-industry-resource-list/

I made mention of **Helen Austin's articles** in this

section, so I thought I would reference them here. For those who are interested in pursuing licensing and placement opportunities, I believe her articles are a great starting point.

- ➤ **4 Steps to Film and TV Placement**

- ➤ **Next Steps to Music Licensing**

- ➤ **7 Steps to Finding a Music Publisher**

4. Adapting, Growing, and Thriving in The Information Age

By most accounts, the music industry has fallen behind the times. I wouldn't say that it has become irrelevant or obsolete, but it seems as though it has been in reactionary mode (and not transition mode) for quite some time.

Perhaps, as an industry, we didn't take the internet seriously enough. It was foolish to think that the Compact Disc would remain a viable business model forever. History showed otherwise. Format shifts have been happening long before we ever had CDs.

And yet, when Napster came along in the 90s, we treated it as an imposter; not a prophet. In hindsight, Napster was signalling the end of an era. It was showing us what was to come, and how music would be marketed and distributed in the **information age**.

I'm sure you can think of a few examples, like iTunes, Pandora or Spotify.

It's easy to remain on the sidelines and criticize, but the reality is that nobody really knew how the internet would change the industry, and ultimately, the world.

The information age is here in full force. What are the implications for the industry at large and for aspiring artists?

Firstly, it's important to recognize that **change is constant**. Changes are coming more rapidly than ever before, and failing to stay current means getting left behind. Though the consequences may not be far-reaching at first, they will catch up with you if you refuse to adapt, like a brick-and-mortar video rental store in the age of Netflix.

Secondly, **change is not indicative of progress**. Whether you are setting goals for your life or building your music career, you have to remember this. Change is needed, but it doesn't automatically translate to *better*.

Thirdly, **traditional jobs are becoming far less relevant**. We've all heard that people, on average, will change careers anywhere from seven to nine times throughout their lifetime. However, the reality is that *job security is all but a thing of the past*. People should not count on it or rely on jobs for their security.

Entrepreneurship and creativity are becoming pre-requisites to life as opposed to privileges of the brilliant or the eccentric. If you play it too safe and count on employment, your insurance plan or the government to support your lifestyle and take care of you for the rest of your life, you will let many opportunities slip by (and that's the *best case scenario*).

I think this is where musicians have a distinct advantage over those who virtually do nothing outside of their nine-to-five working life (not that there's anything wrong with a simple life).

Musicians are already tapped into their creative side, and are learning important problem-solving skills through their career experiences. They are learning to relate to people in their own way. By all accounts, they are better positioned to take advantage of these exciting times.

However, I have also observed that many musicians are sitting in the stands when they should be out on the court getting involved in the game. What I mean is that many musicians are thinking without acting, criticizing without understanding, and judging without experiencing. The peanut gallery has it easy; **they never produce anything worth criticizing**.

When you start doing the work, you will see everything from a whole different vantage point. You will begin to see that great art takes work. I would advise spending less time grumbling and more time creating.

Sure, it's important to develop your critical faculties as a musician. Otherwise, no amount of personal practice will actually bring significant improvement. You have to have a realistic and analytical view of your own abilities if you ever want to become a better instrumentalist and musician than you are now. You have to have self-awareness.

Notwithstanding, I believe musicians have to learn to relinquish their right to elitism, snobbery and to a degree, even skepticism.

Because of the times we live in, we're going to see many new companies emerge in the industry. There are going to be new models of distribution and marketing. There are going to be apps and social platforms that we can't even imagine at this moment in time.

As a musician, you have to do your due diligence in evaluating new opportunities as they come along. Some will be right for you, and some won't. However, it's good to remember that formats will shift again, and trends will dictate the necessity to adopt new technology, like a musician on MySpace that hasn't realized the importance of Facebook yet (although MySpace *has* started to shift with the times too).

It's not that technology runs or determines your career; rather, **you will have to remain open to new developments**. If you want to use social media as a marketing tool, you will have to stay on top of the trends.

Additionally, it won't do you or others much good to be a jerk. Criticism, elitism and snobbery are often the offspring of insecurity. Skepticism is often the by-product of a closed mind. A closed mind probably won't serve you well in the information age.

Navigating this new age will require that you remain open. If you stay open, you might risk making mistakes. If you stay open, you might experience failure from time to time. Even so, if you don't risk, you will have a hard time getting ahead. Playing it safe will not guarantee a safe passage to success. In fact, making **mistakes and failing should be seen as the foundation to eventual success**. If you play it safe, you risk spinning your wheels.

This does not negate the need to be careful. *Of course you should be careful!* You shouldn't make mistakes just because you can. You shouldn't sign agreements that don't make sense for you. Still, you *should* make mistakes early so that you can learn from them and adapt. When nobody knows you, there's no need to be polished. When *everyone* knows you, even smaller slips in integrity could be costly.

I am not about finger-pointing or legalism or fear-mongering. The industry is not in the state it's in because of someone or some entity in particular; we brought it upon ourselves as a collective. But let's move beyond that. Let's learn to make the most of the opportunity at hand. There may be some downsides to being a musician in the information age, but it's also a really exciting time to be pursuing a career in music.

5. Personal Development

 For the best return on your money, pour your purse into your head. - Benjamin Franklin

My personal mission includes **encouraging others to pursue a journey of personal growth** through mentorship, reading stimulating books and listening to inspiring audio. I make it a point to do these things on a daily basis myself.

I felt I had to include a chapter on this subject because I've personally gained a great deal from the reading and studying I've done. I've gained confidence in myself and my abilities. I've started going out of my comfort zone on a regular basis. I've started taking more risks, financially and personally. I've started successful exercise plans and diet habits. I've learned to maximize my productive time. I've improved upon my strengths. I've increased my income. I've negotiated for better terms. The list goes on, and I'm still improving.

This isn't to say that personal growth is a pursuit without an end. Rather, *learning* should be embraced as a lifelong pursuit.

Many years ago, my self-image was in the gutter. My father passed away when I was 13 years old and I think that played a significant part in how I viewed myself. I also modeled myself after other family members who often said self-deprecating or defeatist things and put themselves down (I still love my family though). There was a time when I could barely look people in the eye. I couldn't hold conversations with pretty girls. I didn't date at all until several years after College. However, a lot of that has changed. If there's hope for me, don't ever think there isn't hope for you.

Whatever situation you find yourself in today, you have to start taking responsibility for your life. Having brought up my past, I want to be clear on this point: **personal development is not about playing the victim**. It's about embracing every circumstance in your life.

Some people think personal development is only for the helpless, desperate or depressed; I believe it's for people in pursuit of excellence. You may not start at the same point I did with your self-image. In fact, I hope you don't. If you're starting from neutral, you should be able to grow quicker and faster than I did; and I hope that you do.

Practically speaking, **you can only accomplish what you think is within your capacity**. Personal development will force you to stretch your vision beyond what is comfortable and what you currently think is possible. I think that's important, because, you will only ever see or pursue opportunities that you think you can handle. Subconsciously, you are likely blocking out prospects that you think are beyond your capacity right now.

Furthermore, I wouldn't let other people dictate what is possible for you. When you are personally growing, people may say things like, "Why are you doing *that?*", or "That self-help stuff is stupid, man." Don't worry about them; let them be.

17

If you're reading this, you already *know* you're capable of so much more.

You don't have to take my word for it, but frankly I don't know how you could ever expect to play to a crowd of thousands or tens of thousands of people unless you have a healthy self-image and a vision for it. I don't know how you could go on to sell millions of albums without a personal growth plan. Obviously you don't have to be a special person to make that happen; but if you don't believe it's possible yet, it's time to go to work on yourself. *When you change, your world changes too.* If others can do it, so can you.

I once had a friend who said, "You can't study life. Life will teach you the lessons you need to know." Or rather, *hit you over the head with them at the least opportune moment*! If you approach life that way, you risk having lessons forced upon you. You have to be willing to study, to change and to grow.

At some point, *you* have to take action! Learning in itself won't produce results. *Applying what you learn* will. You will always see life through your own filters. You might have to clean or exchange those filters from time to time.

>> Tools & Tips

To access these and other resources, go to:
http://dawcast.com/the-new-music-industry-resource-list/

- **The Book List:** I've been compiling a list of the best personal growth (and music marketing) books on my website. There are a lot of great books out there, and I believe reading in general is a value-adding activity, but if you don't know where to start, start here.

- **The Audio List:** like the book list, I've also been compiling a list of the best personal growth audios on my website. Use this resource as a jumping off point.

- **Personal Development:** I've written quite a bit about having the right mindset on my blog. If you're not sure that you want to invest in personal growth material just yet, you can go through this section on my blog at your own leisure, entirely for free.

- **Steve Pavlina: Personal Development for Smart People:** this is where it all started for me. Until I began reading Steve's blog, personal development was a foreign concept to me. You can also use his blog as a jumping off point if you'd like. He will steer you towards many fantastic resources as well.

Introduction to Personal Development

I'm going to keep this section as simple as possible. I believe there are only a few key components to growing yourself. Once you develop and implement personal growth habits into your life, they aren't particularly hard to maintain. Taking action and applying the knowledge is the hard part.

Mentorship

I can't really stress enough the importance of good mentorship. Mentorship can come in many forms; it can come from the people you associate with, the books you read, and the audios you listen to. However, I would also encourage you to find someone (or a few someones) that have some or all of the results you want out of your music career and ask for their guidance. Pick their brains as often as you can.

Success often comes from duplicating what others have already done. You don't have to reinvent the wheel. This doesn't mean that you should try to sound like a successful band you know, because that could have certain drawbacks (oh hi, **Theory of a Nicklefault**), but you will find it prudent to talk to people who have accomplished what you'd like to accomplish and ask them how they did it.

More importantly, learn from their **mindset**. Ask them about their work ethic. Ask them what it took and what they had to sacrifice to get to where they are. See if there are any tweaks you could make to your current strategy based on their answers.

One way to create an opportunity for conversations of this nature is to do (podcast) interviews like I do. It helps to have a place on the web that you're going to publish them to, as it can benefit both you and the interviewee. More on that later.

Unfortunately, I'm not aware of any organized mentorship programs available to musicians (and I don't mean *formal education*). I suppose that doesn't mean that there aren't any, but if you can find someone local to counsel and chat with, that would be ideal. Of course, you can't always find successful people locally. However, asking for mentorship is a form of edification, and when you esteem someone to that degree, they are often honoured to help. In other words, asking shouldn't be the hard part.

If you're not afraid to dig deep, these are some great questions for you to ask your mentor:

1) What sort of work ethic did it take for you to get to where you are today?

2) What did you have to sacrifice in order to pursue your goals and dreams?

3) What price did you pay for the success you have? Did you have to miss important family gatherings, lose sleep, or put off fun activities?

4) Does success look neat and organized, or is it scattered and disjointed?

5) What is your mindset around _____?

Reading Books

Reading books is a key component to personal development. Some people like it, some don't. In either case, you should set yourself a daily or weekly quota (i.e. 10 minutes a day). You can enjoy the benefits of reading even if you don't particularly like the activity. You can get through many books in a year if you just commit to reading a few pages every single day. I have heard that you can become an expert on any subject if you just spend 30 minutes a day learning about it. You won't become an expert overnight, of course, but over time you will have accumulated a great deal of knowledge.

There have been periods in my life where I spent the first hour of my morning reading. These days I spend at least 15 minutes in a book on a daily basis. That gets me through one book a month on average. If you're a faster reader, you will likely be able to finish more.

If you have trouble reading some of the classics like *The Magic of Thinking Big* by Dr. David J. Schwartz or *How to Win Friends and Influence People* by Dale Carnegie, you could also spend time in some great music related titles like *How to Promote Your Music Successfully on the Internet* by David Nevue or *All You Need to Know About the Music Business* by Donald S. Passman.

New input can stimulate inspiration and new ideas. Even reading on an unrelated subject can prove beneficial to your creativity. Don't underestimate the benefits of reading on a subject that you don't know anything about; especially if you are experiencing a dip in creativity or writer's block.

Listening to Audio

Much like personal development books, personal development related audio programs aren't hard to find. In some cases, you can also get various book titles in audio form.

They say the average person drives roughly 500 hours a year. If you took that time to proactively listen to audio that could benefit your life and career, where do you think you would be?

Podcasts are also good, not to mention **free**. Listening to people like Seth Godin or Derek Sivers could have tremendous value. *Inside Home Recording*, *CD Baby DIY Musician Podcast* and *Music Career Juice* also contain great information.

I personally listen to at least 30 to 60 minutes of audio every day. This is a bit of a weird habit for a musician to absorb, because if you are anything like I was, I listened to a lot of music in my car. It was my education. There's nothing wrong with that. However, in addition to that, you should also be actively listening to audio to grow yourself and your music career.

Setting Goals

Get good at setting goals and actually following through on them. My good friend Daniel Guy Martin talked about this in episode 11 of my podcast. He worked on an acoustic instrumental album that he had nine weeks to write, record, manufacture and sell 1,000 units. When all was said and done, he achieved his goal!

Charles A. Coonradt's *The Game of Work* has one of the best goal-setting models I have seen to date. To summarize his points:

1) **You must write down your goals**: they are virtually pointless if you don't. Writing down your goals increases your chances of actually achieving them. Yes, use pen and paper.

2) **You must take ownership of your goals**: in context of Coonradt's book, he is talking about employees and corporate situations. In other words, an employee must take ownership of their role in their company and determine what their goals should be. Taking ownership of your role means taking responsibility for your actions; that's one of the best things you can do for yourself. Take ownership of your band and you music career.

3) **Your goals must be positive**: Coonradt gives the example of a smoker who wants to quit. He suggested to his friend that - instead of setting the goal of "quitting" - he should track the exact number of cigarettes he smoked in day, committing to reduce by only one on a daily basis. By the time his friend started implementing this strategy, he was ready to reduce his habit much quicker. Ultimately, this method did achieve the desired outcome; his friend was able to quit

smoking. "Quit smoking" is a negative goal. "Smoke x number of cigarettes today" is a positive goal.

4) **Your goals must be measurable and specific**: you need to set a timeline on your goals, and you need to define a specific number or quantity.

5) **The terms of your goals must be inflation-proof**: in short, your goal should be something that can be measured with the same stick today, tomorrow, next week, next month or next year (arguably, this can be a little tricky when discussing certain items like monetary figures; think instead of the number of shows you've played in year, just as an example).

6) **Your goals must be stated in visible terms**: measuring your goals is easier when you're working with things you can see, feel and touch.

7) **Your goals must have deadlines**: I have heard Japanese pop singer Aska say about one of his albums that he wished he had more time to spend in the studio. In the same breath, he noted that things only seemed to get done *within* the confines of time and deadlines. You have to know *when* you intend to reach your goal.

8) **You need to know why**: *making more money* is a pointless goal unless you know how you're going to spend it. In the same way, goals only matter when you know the *why* behind them. You need to know what

you're going to do with that extra money when you get it.

9) **You must reward yourself**: rewarding yourself after completing a goal isn't merely about going for dinner, buying a new CD or video game, or taking a vacation. It's about the feeling of victory you have as result of accomplishing your goal and ingraining that victory deep within your mind. If you can stack wins, it gets easier to get more of them.

10) **Your goals must be realistic and obtainable**: Don't set goals that are too lofty or out of reach right now. Find a goal that feels realistic and achievable now, and then challenge yourself little by little.

Going to Conventions

Undoubtedly there are benefits to attending conventions, seminars and workshops that are and *aren't* of a personal growth nature. Getting out of your usual mode of operation can help bring clarity and perspective back to your career activities; especially if you go to a convention outside of your own hometown. It enables you to get out of the rut of your usual routine, and perhaps it will inspire you to try some new things or *try the same things in a different way*.

Conventions aren't always for *learning* as much as they are for *making decisions*. Although I would recommend letting the atmosphere and speeches and people *influence* you, I wouldn't be inclined to *change everything you're doing right now*, unless you determine that you're not doing anything productive to move your career forward.

I can remember one function I went to where the panellists and speakers were all made up of people that had established some level of prominence locally, but in essence weren't much further along than anyone else in the room. Although it is always important to listen with humility and understand where the speakers are coming from, you also need to know that they don't always have the ability to steer you in the right direction.

You have to follow your gut. Only you can make accurate decisions that are going to move your career forward. Others can make observations and suggestions, but at the end of the day, you have to know what's right for *your* career. Otherwise, you won't make the sacrifices that need to be made. You won't make the decisions that will help you to experience progress.

This isn't to say that you shouldn't be teachable. You should definitely go to every function with an open mind. You should listen to what others are saying. However, they will likely have a bias towards a particular product or social network or movement because they found a tool that works for them (or they serve to profit from it; but let's think the best of people). You may find that other tools work well for you. You may find that their methods don't really make sense for you based on what you are trying to accomplish.

Moreover, conventions can definitely be a great place to network, to learn about the latest technology, and to *embed in the scene*. If you keep showing up, regardless of the situation, people will begin to recognize you.

There are few people who are born social butterflies, but you will definitely want to learn to be outgoing, available and sociable. This is another area where personal growth might play a part. Music business is a people business. If that doesn't sit well with you, just remember that *every business is a people business*. I know you'd probably rather just focus on the creative side of things, but if you don't become the best representative for your music that you can be, no one else will do it for you.

I will admit that attending conventions is something I hadn't done enough of as an independent artist. I've been to numerous guitar workshops, singer/songwriter circles or other informal gatherings, but if I had to do it all over again I would probably go to more events. I would try to find a major convention that I could go to every quarter.

14 Keys to Personal Growth

Though I may repeat a few points here, I'd like to summarize the key personal development concepts I've unpacked in this chapter. It's always good to review and reinforce. Additionally, there may be a few points that I've only hinted at; they are explained in more detail here.

1) **Seek mentorship**: look for people that have what you want out of life and counsel with them. Ask them pertinent questions and pick their brain. Study their habits and evaluate how you can incorporate them into your own activities.

2) **Read books:** get in the habit of reading books (15 minutes or a single chapter) on a daily basis. It doesn't matter if the reading material is personal growth or music career oriented. You may discover that reading about subjects you know nothing about can inspire you creatively and help you to get out of ruts. Additionally, **some of the best ideas are stored in books**. Don't deprive yourself of good input.

3) **Listen to audio:** again, it doesn't matter if it is personal growth or music career oriented, but you should make it a point to listen to an audio program or a podcast for 30 to 60 minutes daily. The important part is that you engage in wholesome, uplifting, positive programs that *help you*. Find audios that encourage, motivate and inspire you.

4) **Go to conventions:** as a musician, you have to put yourself out there. Motivational seminars, music conventions and even workshops, Meetup groups and social clubs could prove invaluable to your personal growth. You can build your network at these events too. When you see and meet the kind of people that have become successful, you will probably begin to realize that they aren't that much different from you. This should serve to help you build your self-belief.

5) **Invest in yourself:** at first, it might feel weird to invest so much time and money into your personal development. However, if you truly have the desire to help others, you have to be able to help yourself first. If you invest in

yourself, it will ultimately be others that benefit from it. As a side note, if you own a business, personal development materials can generally be written off as tax deductions as well. I'm not a financial tax adviser, so make sure to seek professional advice and do your research before claiming anything as a deduction.

6) **Set goals:** set goals that feel right to you. Don't aspire to things that don't fulfill you. Don't go after objectives that don't get you excited. Oftentimes, people find it helpful to **set goals that feel a little challenging but don't seem out of reach**. Find that balance and continue to replace old goals with new ones as you achieve. The process of achieving smaller, more manageable goals will boost your confidence and help you to accomplish bigger objectives later. Don't forget to *write them down*!

7) **Stay teachable:** I am convinced that you *can* control how teachable you are at any given moment, and, your teachability will determine your willingness to learn, grow and change. This might sound simplistic, and it might even sound cliché. However, I can't emphasize this point enough. Allow me to share a story with you. There is a video on YouTube called "Joe Satriani's Guitar Tips". Before I knew anything about teachability, I watched the video and took away about three tips that I deemed useful to me at the time. Later, in a more teachable state, I came back to the same video and took away 30 tips! When you are teachable, you will get more out of the advice your mentor gives you. You will get more out of every book you read, every speech

you listen to, and every convention you go to. The more teachable you are, the more you are going to learn from this guide.

8) **Develop consistency:** many of us underestimate the power of habit. Our human nature causes us to expect big breakthroughs and instant gratification, but the paradox is that *everything worthwhile takes effort*. Consistent, daily effort is the secret to adulthood. It isn't terribly sexy, but in the long run, a consistent amount of time invested into personal growth on a daily basis will get you to where you want to go. Comedian Jerry Seinfeld was said to have printed out a year-at-a-glance calendar and made it a point to write a joke every single day, whether it was good or not. He would then check off every day that he wrote a joke on his calendar. Then he made it his goal *not* to break **the chain**. It's a simple thing, but it's the simple things that set apart successful people.

9) **Remain patient:** in personal growth, you will have to exercise patience. You've developed a variety of neural pathways that have been ingrained through habit. Some habits have benefited you, while others have held you back. The good news is that you can change your habits. Your brain is wired to help you develop these habits, so as you consciously develop more positive behaviours, you will become more productive and efficient in life too.

10) **Believe:** I think that there is something magical about belief. It can mean the difference between action and

inaction. When you believe in yourself and your dreams, you will begin to act more confidently. Almost involuntarily, you will start doing the things that have a bearing on the future of your career. Such is the power of the subconscious mind. Conversely, if you don't believe, you may not do what is required of you to make progress. Change is automatic, but progress is not.

11) **Learn from your mistakes:** not learning from your failures is the only real mistake you *can* make. In other words, failure is inevitable. What most people fail to do is reflect on their failures. They don't take the time to think about and assess what went wrong, and how they could change to become better-adjusted individuals. Allow your mistakes to teach you.

12) **Document your journey:** documenting your journey is going to make several of the steps on this list a lot easier. For example, journaling about your failures is going to help you find the lessons in them more easily. Documenting your progress is going to help you find the rewards in your journey more readily. One way you can do this is by keeping a log in Evernote, creating a note for every new week or every new day. You could use a spreadsheet to track your activities. You could use a paper agenda or a diary. Logging your life isn't necessarily the most pleasurable activity, so find a method that works for you and stick with it.

13) **Take action:** successful people are those that take action. From harmful emotions to analysis paralysis, there are a whole host of things that hold people back from taking chances. However, it usually comes back to thought. For example, if you have a tendency of thinking that everything you do turns out horribly, you will begin to justify it with your experiences, either because you get in the habit of defeating your own efforts, or you've wired your brain only to pick up on things that *do* turn out horribly. In life, you will often have to act in spite of an apparent lack, whether that lack is time, resources, or energy. It's good to have big dreams, but you need to start where you are with what you have. You need to start adding value to yourself and to other people *now*!

14) **Celebrate the reward:** sometimes, you have to *recognize the reward*. What this means is that - at times - your growth *is* the reward. Unless you stop to think about the person you are becoming on your personal growth journey, you may feel as though you aren't making any progress. Moreover, progress usually isn't measured in days, weeks, or months. It's measured in *years*; years of diligence and consistency. You have to remember that no one is perfect, and no one *becomes* perfect. That isn't really the goal of personal growth. The goal is to become someone who is capable of adding more value to the world. This isn't to say that some rewards of personal growth aren't more readily apparent. Just remember to celebrate your wins, however big or small.

Conclusion

Like a wood chopper that sharpens his axe, you will likely discover that sharpening your mind and growing personally will prepare you for what's ahead. A wood chopper that doesn't stop to sharpen his axe is begging to work harder and longer than the one who is diligent in the maintenance and care of his tools. In other words, when you sharpen your mind, your personal efficiency will begin to increase. You will accomplish more in less time. You will learn to deal with challenges and difficulties with more ease, and you will become more growth-oriented.

Many of us are goal-oriented. As I pointed out earlier, setting goals should definitely be a priority of yours. However, the objective of goal-setting is ultimately personal growth. You will often have to stretch yourself to reach your goals, which means that you *will* grow in the process. It's a good idea to put your focus on growth rather than metrics, numbers or a dollar amount. I have not found dollar figures to be particularly motivating, though that is something you are going to discover for yourself.

What I Like

- ➤ **Audible:** Audible is a great place to access a variety of different audiobooks. It is a service with a cost attached to it, but they also have free offers that you can take advantage of.

- ➤ **YouTube:** it's pretty astounding how much content you can find on YouTube these days. Though it might take a little bit of digging, you can definitely find some great personal development audios and videos.

To access these and other resources, go to: http://dawcast.com/the-new-music-industry-resource-list/

What I Don't Like

To be honest, there isn't too much I don't like about personal growth. However, there are definitely some challenges associated with it, such as:

> **Growing pains:** intentional personal growth will stretch you, which means that you will likely experience some "growing pains" along the way. I think this is likely one of the reasons why people shy away from personal growth. They read a book or two or they listen to an audio and instead of feeling motivated or inspired, they begin to see the gap (and thus the pain) between where they are and where they could be or where they want to be. You have to keep in mind that this is where we all start. You can only rise to become the person you want to be if you have a clear end goal in mind. Growth is always outside of your comfort zone.

> **Early mornings:** you may have heard before that successful people are generally early risers. I liken getting up early to exercise; I don't like doing it, but I like the benefits of it. Former CD Baby founder Derek Sivers often advised musicians to get up an hour earlier. I have to admit, that extra hour does make a huge difference. You still need rest and you still need sleep, but the early

part of your day is always more productive than the latter part. Moreover, don't be afraid of paying the price to accomplish your goals. Sometimes rising early is exactly what you need to do to firm up a gig or a contract. One of the funny things about personal growth is that as you keep studying and you become more excited, you may have a harder time sleeping at night. The bottom line here is that people with goals and dreams become so fired up about realizing their desires that they can hardly sleep. This seems to come with the territory.

> **Networking:** okay, here is one thing I definitely *don't* like. I love people. I love building relationships. However, I don't trust too many people that say they are networkers. Yes, there are definitely those that know a lot of people and genuinely try to connect them in meaningful ways. Anna, my co-host on the podcast, is like that. However, there are also people that just seem to be out to *get something*. I'm sure you've experienced this yourself. A few deeper relationships are always more valuable than many shallow ones.

Action Steps

> **Find a mentor:** a mentor doesn't necessarily have to be a real-life person. You can learn and grow from reading books and listening to value-adding audio. However, if you can take it a step further and interview experts or connect with a local person that you respect, that is ideal.

- ➤ **Acquire personal growth materials:** you've invested in this book. Therefore, it shouldn't be too much of a stretch to purchase other books or audiobooks that are going to help you grow. Scan the lists I've provided you with (**The Book List** and **The Audio List**), and find some other materials that appeal to you.

- ➤ **Set goals:** set goals, and actually write them down. Put them into solid, concrete terms.

- ➤ **Research conventions:** begin to look for conventions locally and across the country. Identify a few that you could see yourself going to every year. Then, begin to plan your schedule around them.

6. Business Mentality

 The cover-your-butt mentality of the workplace will get you only so far. The follow-your-gut mentality of the entrepreneur has the potential to take you anywhere you want to go or run you right out of business - but it's a whole lot more fun, don't you think? - Bill Rancic

Do music and business really go together, as in "music business"?

The short answer is "Yes", and frankly I don't know how else you could make it in music today. Whether you find someone to work the business side for you or you do it yourself (which will likely be the case early on), you'll want to understand the ins and outs of what this means for you and your band (whether or not you're in a band). People often say "work within your strengths", but I'm a believer in developing skills that move you forward, even if those aren't your greatest strengths.

I feel that the creative side and business side of music are less removed from each other than musicians tend to think they are. Business can and should be fun, and that's what's going to attract people to you and your music.

You have to believe in your own music enough to want to promote it. You have to create your own opportunities. You can't count on someone to come along and make everything right. You can't wait for the phone to ring. You should seek meaningful partnerships, but don't wait for the silver bullet. There is no cure-all.

Business mentality has brought great clarity to my own efforts, and I can't imagine not sharing what I've learned so far. I'm not a consummate business professional by any means, though I do aspire to be better every day.

Introduction to Business Mentality

Until I learned business principles, my music career efforts were scattered and unfocused. I chose to avoid difficult situations instead of confronting them. I spread myself entirely too thin. I would *wait* to be motivated instead of *creating* motivation within myself.

It took me a long time to realize this, but *when you understand business mentality, you understand success principles*.

Professionalism

Even as a musician, professionalism is important.

Do you have to wear a suit, carry a briefcase and slick your hair back to be in the music business? Absolutely not. There are plenty of successful industry people who wear casual clothing on their respective jobsites. As a musician, you get a pass in this area. However, that doesn't mean that you shouldn't *conduct and present yourself professionally*.

There are situations where it's inappropriate to ask for someone's opinion on your music. There are situations where it's inappropriate to call or email. Different industry people have different preferences for communication. Try to be mindful of that. Always observe guidelines, especially those that can be easily found on websites.

You will make some mistakes, and that's perfectly okay. You don't have to know all of the rules before you begin. Just remember to study and learn as you go.

As a creative person, I found myself prone to mood swings, and this was a bit of a problem in developing relationships. I would get discouraged and taken out all too easily by setbacks. You'll have bad days for sure, but you're in the music industry because *you believe in your own ability to succeed*. You can't let one or 10 or 100 or even 1,000 setbacks stop you. You have to remember that. If you wind up having a string of negative interactions in one sitting, try to end on a positive one.

Accountability is also a big deal. If you intend to be successful, don't be flaky. Be a person who can and will call if they're running behind or something comes up. Let your word be your bond. Show up when you say you'll show up. Deliver the product at the price you said you would. Be open for business seven days a week. Don't close down. Don't over-commit yourself; you'll find it challenging to deliver what you said you would if you add too much to your plate.

Also, make sure to take care of your personal hygiene. First impressions may not be everything, but it does count, and you want to make a good impression wherever and whenever you're meeting people. Remember to have a firm handshake.

Finally, remember to **be relevant**. I don't respond to emails that say, "Dear site owner, we think you have a really great project here, and think our services could help you." My name is plastered *all over* my website. If they can't even get *that* right, why do I owe them a response? Keep in mind who you're talking to, what they do, and why you're reaching out to them.

Finances

When it comes to finances, I believe it's important to create a separate chequing account for your music. That's the first step. The second step is learning to put away every cent you earn from gigs, merch, royalties and music sales. It's tempting and sometimes hard to avoid spending it on alcohol and/or fried foods after a show. However, money is necessary to sustain a music career. *Music costs money*. Recording costs money, replication and printing costs money, radio campaigns cost money and touring can – unfortunately – cost money.

It is absolutely possible to make money in music, so don't misunderstand me when I say this. However, the sooner you learn to properly manage your finances, the better off you will be.

As an aside, when I still owned a home, roughly $3,000 - $4,000 would fly out of my bank account every month. Maybe it would spring you to action, but I found that it took up way too much of my mind space. It was not motivating. It was hard to think clearly, and I would busy myself with too many projects. Lack of focus was the bane of my existence.

Learn to be frugal, especially in the beginning stages. Selling my house and moving into a basement suite was quite possibly the best decision I've ever made in recent years. I have a lot of peace, and I don't really think about money as much anymore. Alas, I don't have much of a home studio at this time (I do have all the gear and the ability to record), but the positive has definitely outweighed the negative.

There's a word for this: it's called *streamlining*. When I say **be frugal**, there may be some (in some cases *many*) unnecessary expenses in your life that you could cut back on. You could disconnect your cable TV. You could stop eating out. You could buy cheaper food. I think a lot of people avoid taking this step because they think it's going to be a permanent arrangement. *It doesn't have to be.* As your influence and income increases, you can increase your lifestyle again. However, I would never recommend doing this too quickly. Get comfortable with delaying gratification.

Long-Term Commitment

Give your music career five to 10 years of **consistent** effort (and be *willing* to go even longer). There's no magical reason for the number, but there are many examples of bands (like Billy Talent or Metallica) that didn't make it until close to (or until after) the 10 year mark. Moreover, it's a matter of commitment. If you're going to put a band together, you'll want to find people who can (and will) actually keep at it for that length of time.

This is also common business practice. It often takes about five years for an upstart company to be profitable. I believe the reason for this is that one's dedication has to be tested. If it was easy to succeed, everyone would already be successful. It takes perseverance. You have to keep putting in the work to build the foundation, even when nothing seems to be happening.

I have been in a couple of bands in which I thought all the members were committed, but in those cases I eventually found out that I was wrong. I took their words at face value. That may not have been wise. If you trust someone's words, you could be disappointed. Watch a person's actions and you will never be confused. I hope that doesn't sound too cynical, but if I had to do it all over again, I would have found *committed people*, even over *talented people*. We live in a day and age where people with marketable skills are sometimes (often) coming out on top of talented people.

However, there is no "perfect" situation. Some people will come, and some will go. Don't try to hold on to them. Instead, do your best to maintain a group of people who together have a common interest in realizing a vision. Create a support group around yourself.

Sacrifice

Here's a dose of realism; you can't be too scared of losing a little sleep, giving up some television or cutting back on your spending *if you intend to be successful*. Most if not all successful people have sacrificed for a window of time (also note what I said about *streamlining*). It has to be for a purpose worth pursuing, or you may lose momentum. You have to be clear about your motivation. Your *why* is more important than your *what* or your *how*.

I think Larnell Lewis spoke beautifully to this point on the podcast (to access this resource, go to: **http://dawcast.com/the-new-music-industry-resource-list/**).

As for me, among other things, I gave up cable TV. That wasn't really a hard decision. A lot of people watch TV and believe they are gaining *useful knowledge*. The average person in North America today watches something like five to six hours of TV *every single day*. If everyone's doing it and getting practically the same results, it couldn't possibly be a good source of information, could it?

Do you really think that hitting the pubs and hanging out every weekend is going to earn you your financial freedom? Do you think that playing it safe is going to make you a cut above average? Do you think that watching TV will actually equip you with the knowledge, wisdom and information you need to make good decisions for your career? You need to get real with yourself.

Consistency

Momentum is difficult to build, especially on spurts of effort (even if those spurts are substantial). *Momentum is a by-product of consistency and regularity*. In other words, a little bit of effort on a daily basis is better than random and disjointed capsules of labour. That's how pretty much everything works in life. You probably didn't get good at your instrument by practicing for seven hours once. You improved gradually and progressively through daily effort. If you're willing to do this to learn an instrument, you should also be willing to do it for the future of your career. You should be willing to do it for your business.

15 Principles of Entrepreneurship

As a musician, you are essentially an entrepreneur already. You have to find your own gigs, and you have to market and sell your own music, that is, unless someone else is already helping you out with it. If you are just starting out, chances are pretty good that you're the one wearing all the hats.

One of the things I talk about on my blog as well as my podcast is **music entrepreneurship**. In essence, it's the idea that there are many different ways of funding your music career. You probably know many musicians who work a day job to support their career. There's nothing wrong with that, but you should be aware that there are alternatives.

Just because the people you know are doing it a certain way doesn't mean that you have to follow suit. You're allowed to break the mould, though undoubtedly it will take some courage, and it might even look a little risky at first.

A musician who has been brought up in a traditional home will think, "You *have* to have a job."

Nonsense. You don't *have* to do anything. You don't have to go to college, you don't have to play it safe, and you certainly don't have to do what everyone else is doing just because it's popular. You *can* be successful without all of the trappings that many people think are pre-cursors to winning in life.

"Are you suggesting I go broke?"

Why in the world would I suggest that? I already mentioned the fact that debt is a killer. I went into depth about the importance of managing your finances.

The point is that entrepreneurs are problem-solvers, and they tend to see things a little differently than others.

For example, you *could* build a business on the side that funded your passion for music. You *could* streamline your lifestyle to the point where you worked very little or not at all. You might even be able to stay in a friend's cabin for a few months and practice all day long.

However, if you're not in the problem-solving mindset, you won't see these possibilities. You do whatever people tell you to do because it sounds sensible. Should I point out the irony? A music career is just about the furthest thing from *sensible*!

I'm not telling you what to do. It's *your* music career, and you have to make decisions that feel right to you. I am simply stating the fact that there are some advantages to seeing the possibilities and alternatives in every situation.

So, if entrepreneurship sounds like something you want to pursue further, here are some key principles that will help you.

1) **Add value:** the foundation of entrepreneurship is **value**. An entrepreneur does not get wealthy making junk;

they get wealthy helping and serving others in the world. They add value to them. Sure, there are those that take advantage of people and give the title a bad name, but wouldn't you say it's the same in the music business? I'm sure you can think of *a few* people you don't particularly care for right now. Besides, I don't see music as being any different. Musicians also become successful by adding value. Fundamentally, the value of music lies in how it makes people *feel*. You could break that down into a lot of smaller items like community, a sense of belonging, connection, but in essence it all comes back to **feeling**. Additionally, there *are* other ways of adding value to people. Your music is a good place to start, but it should extend out into your relationships, your shows, your products and your communication.

2) **Treat others with respect:** this goes for anyone you work with or come in to contact with, be it band members, fans, or record executives. If I was playing in a band again, I wouldn't worry too much about alienating large groups of people. Some people will be interested in your personality and music, and others won't. You can't get too caught up in trying to please everyone. Personally, I would be more concerned with keeping a good reputation and treating others well. Sure, nice people don't get talked about as much as the jerks, but word travels fast when you're a jerk. It's like a bad customer experience; people tend to tell between nine to 15 other people when they've had a less-than satisfactory consumer experience. People may not

always share a good experience, but if you're nice to people, at least you're not in danger of creating a bad reputation that precedes you wherever you go. Most importantly, always remember to **treat your fans with respect**. They are the ones supporting you. They are the ones coming to your shows, buying your CDs and your merchandise, and they are the ones that will enable you to create a sustainable career. Be okay with your customers (especially *paying* customers) being right; you wouldn't have a career without them.

3) **Commit:** an entrepreneur has to stay focused and committed to their projects if they want to see any kind of success. If they don't monitor their progress, they may end up making costly mistakes that could have been avoided. However, cultivating focus is easier said than done. I should know. I'm the guy with seven websites to maintain. Again, there is a parallel here with music. It's hard to achieve success unless you're committed. Business is not about putting out fires; it's *all* a big fire! If you want to stay in the game and play, you're going to have to come to terms with the fact that there will be challenges. Do keep in mind, however, that challenges always present you with the opportunity to grow. Don't underestimate the power of a challenge to stretch your capacity.

4) **Develop your leadership:** a good entrepreneur knows how to lead people. This isn't to say that every successful entrepreneur ever in existence has been a tactful and caring leader. However, they are willing to

set the pace for their team, and they work to become the best possible example they can be. Are you the leader of your band? If so, you have to be willing to set the pace. No one is going to work as hard as you, and no one is going to care as much as you do. If you're lucky, your team will do *about* the same amount of work as you, but in most cases, they will do less. Make sure your example is one that's worth following. How do you develop your leadership? Read the preceding chapter on personal development.

5) **Persist:** entrepreneurs know that most undertakings require long-term commitment. They know that there will be ebbs and flows with any venture, and they are prepared to work and persist through them. Do you understand the difference between this mindset and an entitlement mindset? Do you see how meeting challenges with the right attitude would allow one to work through them with more ease? Whether you're a solo artist or you play with a band, there will likely be personal, relational and business challenges. Are you willing to persist in the face of resistance?

6) **Stay flexible:** entrepreneurs aren't always able to nail down every detail in their business ventures. Oftentimes, this is just the nature of running a business. Entrepreneurs have to remain open to the possibilities and be willing to embrace the opportunities they are presented with. They know that their vision may not come to fruition exactly the way they imagine it. They know that God or the Universe might bring it about

another way, so they stay alert and keep an eye on the radar. Is failure also a possibility? Of course, but entrepreneurs are quick to find the lesson, learn it, and get back up. As a musician, you have to be open to the possibility that your music will reach an audience you never thought it would. You have to be open to the possibility that making a small tweak to your sound could mean the difference between a small, uncaring audience and a large, enthusiastic one! The little things do count.

7) **Embrace failure:** if you consider yourself an entrepreneur, you can't be too afraid of making mistakes. Certainly, some are more costly than others. However, in every failure there is also a lesson. There is an opportunity to learn and grow. It may seem counterintuitive, but the foundation for success is paved by a trail of failures. If all you do is tread carefully, analyze every situation and try to manage risk, it's hard to move forward. It may seem easier, but you rarely if ever encounter headwinds if you're not trying to change. It's when you're pushing through the resistance that the greater challenges come. There is something to be said for mitigating risk, to be sure (you have to bring your brain with you), but analysis paralysis is far more detrimental over the long haul. As a musician, you will experience some failure. Just remember that every failure *can* be a stepping stone to greater achievement. However, you still have to *choose* it.

8) **Embrace uncertainty:** entrepreneurs don't always know how things are going to turn out. Nevertheless, they embrace the uncertainty in their business ventures. They are seemingly self-assured, even when turbulence is manifesting all around them. They have come to the understanding that bumpy roads are merely indicators of growing pains. Easier said than done? Indeed, it is. However, if you want to be a leader, you have to remain stable. Pay attention to your self-talk and the words you speak. They possess more power than you even realize. Pay attention to your inner world; ensure that you don't lose hope. As a musician, you may find yourself in situations where you don't know where the next paycheck or gig is going to come from. Learn to see the possibilities around you.

9) **Experiment:** just because entrepreneurship involves business doesn't mean that it has to be stuffy or boring. In fact, it *should* be fun and exciting! Your journey is what you make of it; you *can* learn to laugh in the face of adversity. It is possible to approach business playfully. An entrepreneur knows that there could be valuable ideas and lessons hidden within every "diversion". They know the value of experimentation. Here, too, there is a meaningful parallel to music. Just think of Carl Douglas and his hit, "Kung Fu Fighting". Originally, it was going to be a B-side to "I Want to Give You My Everything". "Kung Fu Fighting" was a silly, fun song that was recorded in 10 minutes, and yet, today, it is far more recognized than "I Want to Give You My Everything". Don't be too

quick to dismiss seemingly silly ideas; you might have something valuable on your hands!

10) **Understand the risks:** understanding the risks is generally more about developing good sense than it is about investing a lot of time and energy into investigating every divergent path. I was going to use the term "common sense", but entrepreneurship tends to challenge the status quo, so it didn't sound quite right. While there will always be some risk associated with creative ventures, also know that there is greater long-term risk that results from **inaction**. In the long run, entrepreneurship is more secure than traditional employment. They just don't teach you that in school. I previously noted that learning from your mistakes is more important than mitigating them, and I still believe that to be the case. However, like I said before, you shouldn't make mistakes just because you can. Make it a point to avoid the *same* mistakes; that's how you know you're progressing.

11) **Adapt:** entrepreneurs have to be willing to adapt. Technology continues to change at a rapid pace, and as result, business practices also change. In the short term, that may not wreak havoc on a business. In the long run, it could prove *catastrophic*. Think about it. Format shifts have changed the way people consume music. If you were still selling tapes, though you might have a small buying audience, you would probably be leaving a lot of money on the table too. Likewise, when MySpace took a nosedive into oblivion, a lot of people migrated over to

Facebook. You could have stayed on MySpace and kept a small following, but you probably would have found more traction with Facebook. Who knows what the format or social media platform of tomorrow will be, but remember to stay flexible.

12) **Take responsibility:** an entrepreneur is willing to take responsibility for results, or the lack thereof. There is something amazing that happens when a person begins to take responsibility for their life. They are able to turn their life around for the better very quickly. Again, this goes contrary to popular belief. A lot of people avoid responsibility, because they are afraid of the implications. Not many people know how truly empowering it is to know that everything in your life is a result of your own thinking and actions. As it pertains to entrepreneurship, taking responsibility is one way of "mitigating" risk. When you are willing to take the heat for the bad and give credit away for the good, you are becoming a first-class leader.

13) **Know the score:** success and failure are pretty obscure terms unless you have a way of defining them. An entrepreneur keeps an eye on the score at all times, and they don't make it a point to trust terms like "a little" or "a lot". For example, two complaints should not be considered a *lot* of negative feedback. Entrepreneurs work to keep an honest and balanced perspective on the metrics so that they know what action to take next. Similarly, you can't have an accurate view of your music marketing efforts unless you have numbers to back it

up. In the online marketing world, this is pretty easy because you can use tools like Google Analytics to track your website stats. Facebook and other social networks automatically logs detailed information on how your posts are engaging. It can be a little more challenging in the offline world, but with a little effort, you can track things like merchandise sales and concert attendance. In the end, it isn't all about the numbers, but they can be used to help you balance your outlook.

14) **Create a plan:** nobody, no matter how successful, had a perfect plan when they were first getting started in business or music. Therefore, you don't *need* a perfect plan. What you need is a guide that outlines your vision, your focus and your goals. If your goals can be broken down into smaller action steps, you have a plan that's worth following. *The plan that you start with is not the plan that will get you there*. You will have to make some changes along the way, and that's perfectly fine.

15) **Create a long-term vision:** entrepreneurs always have a long-term vision for their business ventures. They have a specific end result in mind, and daily work towards its achievement. This makes a lot of sense, because *if you don't plan, you're planning to fail*. Entrepreneurs *begin* with a picture of success. That allows them to make the decisions that will get them to where they want to go. They are also committed to their projects over the long term. They don't discount the possibility that they could reach their goals sooner than expected, but they also don't *count* on it. Do you have a

long-term vision for your music career? Do you know where you want to end up? Are you regularly picturing it in your mind? If not, it's a good time to get started.

Conclusion

If you don't feel like you have it together in the area of business, don't worry. They don't generally teach this stuff in school. Moreover, I knew very little about business or enterprise until 2011, and I am still in the process of learning!

Don't feel discouraged or overwhelmed; I have yet to meet a single person who executes perfectly. That's not the point. The point is to begin to see how applying business principles to your music can benefit you.

Legalism and perfectionism doesn't serve anyone. At the very least, I know that it doesn't serve me. Business can oftentimes sound like a lot of "do-this" and "don't-do-that" ultimatums, when in reality, very few people can actually give you a tempered and balanced view of how they achieved what they achieved. They may think it was one thing, while it was actually something else. They may think it was a single thing they did that got them to where they are, when in reality it might be *everything* they did.

Don't forget that you have to be the one to call the shots. No one else can tell you what's right for you.

What I Like

➢ **Long-term vision**: the sooner you realize that consistent, daily effort is required of you, the sooner you can embrace the process. We've all heard that *Rome was not built in a day*. It takes time to accomplish anything worthwhile. Creating a long-term vision has helped me to appreciate my daily actions a little more. Though breakthroughs are nice when they happen, as long as you keep your eyes on the vision, even when results don't seem forthcoming, you won't get easily discouraged.

➢ **Financial management:** I rather like the idea of separating your business finances from your personal finances. As long as you are diligent in setting aside every cent you make from music, you can always invest back into your business and career. You will make smarter purchase decisions as a result, too.

➤ **Mint:** if keeping track of your finances seems like a chore and budgeting feels like a slog, Mint (a smartphone app) will automatically log your spending habits for you, and send you weekly email reports. For some, this added layer of accountability should help in controlling spending.

To access these and other resources, go to: **http://dawcast.com/the-new-music-industry-resource-list/**

What I Don't Like

➤ **Legalism:** I already mentioned the fact that I don't like legalism. Successful speakers tend to be pretty convicted about their beliefs, and that is as it should be. However, I have found that what they say *can* be taken the wrong way. Be willing to go a little deeper, and if you have a mentor, talk to them about anything you're struggling with. Journal about anything that really challenged you to figure out why.

➤ **Repeat problems:** chalk this one up to human nature. You could be winning in life, making strides, when all of a sudden you meet an immovable object called **resistance**. We always have a choice to push through, go a different direction, or give up. However, if you just keep changing directions, you can eventually expect to meet with the same challenges. Pushing through is usually the right answer, unless you need to let go of some things to streamline your schedule, in which case, giving up is the right decision.

Action Steps

> **Set up a business chequing account:** I wouldn't necessarily suggest going to your bank to set up a real business account with them. The problem is that you usually end up getting overcharged for these services. See if you can find an institution that offers no-fee bank accounts locally and set up an account with them. You don't need to tell them that you're going to use it for business purposes. Simply do all of your business related transactions through this account.

> **Set aside business income:** get into the habit of depositing your music related income into your "business" account. If you're not in the habit of doing it, it might seem a little weird at first. However, it will come in handy when certain eventualities occur. Maybe you will need to pay your way to a convention. Maybe you will need to put gas in your car to get to the next venue or repair your touring van. You'll be glad you set aside the money when the inevitable happens.

> **Make a plan:** start making a career plan, and make sure to write it down. Don't place any filters on your plan; you don't have to know *how* you're going to achieve everything you intend to. Simply intend to, and allow the paths before you to unfold.

7. Touring & Live Performance

 A lot of people can't stand touring, but to me it's like breathing. I do it because I'm driven to do it. - Bob Dylan

When I was 15 years old, I performed in front of a large audience for the very first time (it was probably no more than 60 to 100 people, but that was sizeable to me at the time). I was at a summer youth camp, and all week long I had been singing and rapping; particularly "Weird Al" Yankovic's "Twister". My friend Nick Mack joined in and fed off of my love of music.

On the last night of that youth camp, there was a talent show. Nick and I were asked to go up and perform "Twister", without a DJ or any backing music. I remember being a little nervous, but we agreed to do it anyway. The emcee (one of the camp counsellors) asked for our names, and he ended up introducing us as Jon & Mike. Oh boy.

Nick and I walked up, did our thing, and when we finished, we started marching out of the building as we had planned. Surprisingly, our performance was met with wild applause.

That's the story of how I got into music. In ensuing years, I wrote songs, I started learning the guitar, I played shows, and I set up a home studio with my friend Adam Burwash. Sure, there may have been other events leading up to that point, but once I had experienced the thrill of live performance (it was like a drug), I *had* to experience it again.

Introduction to Touring

The moment I got involved in a band, I always dreamed of touring. I wanted to travel and expose our music to as many people as possible as soon as possible. Suffice to say, it didn't exactly work out as I thought it would.

I started learning the guitar in 2001. It wasn't until I started playing with a band called Angels Breaking Silence in 2008 that I started getting a taste of what it would be like to be on the road. We played many out-of-town shows, but we never had a string of dates that took us around the province or the country.

In subsequent years, I went on mini tours with my friend Jonathan Ferguson as well. These tours usually lasted a week, and we would play in three or four towns. In between shows, we would rehearse and busk on the streets.

To this day I haven't had the chance to tour in the capacity that I would like to, but I have had a bit of experience. In short, there's only so much I can impart to you. I've studied the topic quite a bit, but some of my thoughts here are simply inference.

Career Paths

At this point I thought I should touch on the idea of **career paths**, at least briefly. Touring is absolutely necessary for a band with major label ambitions. However, there are other profitable routes in the music industry that may not involve as intensive of a traveling and performing schedule. I know people that produce music and perform but also do speaking engagements. I know people that primarily spend their time making music from home and make a living doing it.

Ultimately, you have to decide what *you* want to do. Whether you aim to remain independent or get signed, your goals are *your goals*. Now more than ever, you have the freedom to *choose* a career path in the music industry that matches your goals. Composers and musicians that work exclusively towards getting placements in TV and film can do the bulk of their work from their home studio. Jonathan Coulton, writer of novelty songs, got his start recording and releasing new material on a weekly basis and interacting with his fans for several hours a day. His is not a career path that is entirely tour oriented, but has certainly led to touring opportunities thanks to the popularity of his work.

Work Ethic

I've hinted at this already, but I will spell it out for you: one thing you should know about touring is that labels - both indie and major - are looking for bands with a strong work ethic. They are looking for hardworking bands, and if you're not willing to tour and grind it out on a yearly basis, you are not likely to emerge as a candidate for a record deal. I know I'm repeating myself, but there *are* other career paths and you don't have to make a major label contract a part of your goals. However, if that's what you want, you definitely need to tour.

Making Contact

Obviously there are several different ways of making contact with venues and event planners. Presented here is an analysis of the different ways you can make contact to get booked. Since I've made some glaring blunders in this area, I will be talking a little bit about that, and I will also touch on the various upsides and downsides of each communication method.

1) **Postal mail**: one of the first misguided things I did to try to get one of my band's tour booked was a postal mail blast. The band cleared their schedule for the summer, and we requested bookings to fill up our calendar. I went online to find as many churches I possibly could (maybe not the best strategy) and mailed out a little under 200 letters countrywide. The first thing I didn't really take into account was the fact that mass mailings cost quite a bit of money. It may seem obvious, but *if you're going to plan a postal mail campaign, you better have a budget for it*. Another problem was that we used a form letter for every mailing; no personalization. We did take the time to sign each one, but our letters probably should have been addressed to the proper department and/or people. The result was roughly three responses out of all the letters that went out. One church wanted to book us but kept putting it off until we never heard back. One church ripped our letter, sent it back and wrote something to the effect of, "we don't believe in Rock music." The other church that got back to me was actually a church I attended when I was younger. I got an email from the pastor asking me if I

was the same kid who attended his church when I was younger. I replied "Yes" and never heard back. Additionally, we had 1,500 some odd envelopes addressed to churches across the States ready to be sent out. We never sent them due to budgetary constraints. So, in short, postal mail campaigns can definitely work, but you'll want to be organized. Make sure to address your mail to someone specific, set aside a budget, and target venues you could see your band playing in. Postal mail is also a necessary part of radio campaigns, which I'll get into later.

2) **Email**: I would occasionally get inspired to send out huge numbers of emails to book shows. It may have gotten me a few bit pieces on blogs or the occasional show, but scattered and inconsistent effort didn't seem to pay off. I would suggest narrowing your focus. Figure out where you actually want to play. Try to focus on one or two interactions at a time and see it to completion. Even if the answer is "No" or "Not right now", at least you have an answer. Move to the next venue on your list and see where that interaction takes you. Email can be a very, very effective tool for your music career.

3) **Phone calls**: much like email, I would occasionally feel compelled to make numerous calls at one sitting. This was actually more effective in getting me shows, but again I was not consistent. I would recommend making friends with your phone as soon as you possibly can. Get good at making casual conversation with people

and listen more than you talk. You can always find someone's need/want/desire if they're willing to talk, and you can also find creative ways of solving their problem (i.e. "I've got this event coming up and I'm not sure what kind of entertainment to book."). It won't always be that obvious or directly connected to what you do, but you might be able to put them in touch with someone who can help them. People usually feel obligated to reciprocate, so when you help them out, they'll help *you* out in return (although that shouldn't be your motivation). Phone calls are more personal than emails and can be extremely effective. Just realize that there are some people in the industry who don't want to be contacted by phone because of their busy careers or sheer number of artists they have to deal with. Always observe conduct guidelines and preferences.

4) **Personal contact**: making personal contact was perhaps the most effective means of booking shows for me. It's important to note that there are some cases where venues specifically ask you to contact them by email or phone. Always observe those rules and don't push the issue. I successfully booked many local shows on personal contact, but in my case it did not lead to any tours. Obviously there are certain limitations with making contact in person. You can't realistically book a tour that way, because you can't possibly go and meet every venue owner. That would be like a pre-tour tour! If you're not a people person, practice and learn to be one. Treat every relationship like it's important.

Research

If there's another lesson you could take from my postal mail campaign, it would be that the internet has made research a much easier task than it used to be. I managed to find a database with thousands of church listings and their mailing addresses. I may have been a bit misguided with the *who* and the *how*, but the *what* wasn't completely off-base.

In other words, I should have spent more time thinking about appropriate venues for my band and taking care in addressing the letters and envelopes to the appropriate departments, but the idea itself wasn't all bad. I have chatted with David Hooper who feels that postal mail can be a very effective tool, if for no other reason than the fact that fewer and fewer people seem to be using it.

Take time to research venues. Keep tabs on where other bands you know are performing. Find bands that are in a similar genre as you and contact them. Ask for tips and advice. If you're lucky, you might even wind up with a list of prospective venues or an opening slot!

Working Together

A band that is willing to come together as a team will experience greater success in organizing tours. Don't wait for the silver bullet. Don't wait for the magical day when you find an awesome booking agency or touring manager. Don't wait to get invited on another prominent band's tour. There are no cure-alls. In the music industry, *you have to create your opportunities*, especially as it pertains to touring.

When I was in a band called Angels Breaking Silence, I was in charge of managing the website, the blog, and writing copy. I worked in my strengths. Other band members handled things like social media and street promotion. They worked in their strengths. If you're working as a team, figure out who can do what and keep each other accountable.

Introduction to Live Performance

Obviously, live performance and touring are closely linked together. They are not one and the same, but many of the topics already discussed apply to live performance as much as they do to touring.

Where touring might involve considerable time, energy and travel, live shows can be spread out and booked in any way you want. There are some advantages to this.

Firstly, scheduling the occasional live show allows you to put a lot more thought into it. When you are on the road touring, you have to focus on delivering on your promises and traveling from one town to the next. When you are not under this concerted pressure, you can focus on creating events that are truly memorable for your fans (especially in your hometown).

Secondly, you can create opportunities for experimentation. You could put on a free acoustic show or a collaborative show where you jam with musicians that aren't in your band. These types of shows are easy to coordinate, especially in a venue that does not offer any pay, but does allow you to use their stage. People's expectations won't be as high when they know that there's no pay involved.

Thirdly, you can book a show simply to practice and hone your skills. It may take some time before you are fully comfortable on stage. Every performance will get you closer to where you want to be. If you are still in the "grinding" stage, then have fun with it. Don't put yourself under undue pressure to play a certain number of songs or have a perfect performance.

Whatever your goal, there are few things as powerful as a live performance to create a following. When you take your eyes off of yourself and work towards creating a memorable experience for your fans, it won't be long before more people are coming to see your shows.

Checklists

When you're playing live, you can get wrapped up in the excitement and energy of the show and forget to do what you need to do onstage. Likewise, you could get so wrapped up in practicing and rehearsing for the performance that you forget to pack all of your gear.

Regardless of the situation, here are a few checklists worth creating:

- **Performance checklist**: when performing, I would inevitably forget to do something I intended to do. I would forget to bring my email signup forms. Or, if I had my email list with me, I would forget to bring my camera. I would forget to mention our website or talk about our album. I would forget to let people know about a promotion on Facebook. Then it finally came to me: I should have a performance checklist! This would

67

be a list of important things that you feel you should do at every show. This would include things like plugging your website or letting your fans know about your next show. If you have that checklist in front of you (even if you have to tape it to your snare drum, keyboard or guitar), you'll always remember to let your fans know about the important stuff. If you have a particularly good show, you might regret not letting your fans know about your current merch special, just as an example. Create a document in Google Drive so you can share it with your band members and anyone else that's involved, and print up copies as necessary.

- **Marketing checklist:** this list should be made up of things that you do to market each of your shows. You may even want to create short procedure descriptions for yourself, just in case you forget something or you end up having someone else cover these items on your behalf. This list would include things like social media posting, updating the concert listing on your website, or writing and submitting a press release to promote your show. You can continue to add to this list as you find more ways of promoting your shows.

- **Music gear checklist:** this list might go on the inside of your Rubbermaids or equipment cases. This will come in handy when you are preparing for a show, but it will also prove useful for when you are packing up after. For example, if all of your gear is listed by name, quantity and description, you will know when you are short a cable or DI box.

Venue Considerations

When you are starting out, you'll probably play some dingy bars and small coffee houses. That's fine. You're going to want to hone your craft, and live performance can greatly aid in that process. Don't despise small beginnings.

At some point, however, you're going to want to give more thought to the venues you play in locally, especially as you develop a dedicated fan base. You'll probably want to stop booking shows on the wrong side of town or that place downtown that nobody can get to.

I've heard it said before that putting on a great live show is like **planning a wedding** (find a venue, book it in advance, send out invites, rehearse, etc.). The venue is particularly important, because you want it to be a place where your fans can enjoy themselves and be comfortable. It should have ample parking space, adequate seating, menu items your fans enjoy, etc.

You can play lots of gigs and make a little more money, or you can plan out a couple of big events on a less frequent basis and make it a particularly memorable experience for your fans (which might end up being more profitable too).

Live Music Production

A lot of bands tend not to think about performance production. In other words, the elements of a great show can really be boiled down to a number of principles that every band can apply. Many bands just think it's a fluke when a particularly great show happens, but most of the time, they don't *just happen*.

If you've had a great show, your band's musicality was probably tight, but more importantly, you probably had a comfort and ease about being on stage that night. You likely upped your stage presence game, even if you were unaware of it. My tip here is to delve into live music production. I have a link to Onstage Success (affiliate link) on my toolbox page, and I would encourage you to take a look at the material they have to offer (To access these and other resources, go to: **http://dawcast.com/the-new-music-industry-resource-list/**). You can greatly increase the effectiveness of your live shows by implementing their methods.

How to Create an Unforgettable Live Experience

How you present your live show is subservient to a few different factors: the size of the venue, the number of people you're playing to, the resources available to you, and so forth.

As you are just starting out, *you will have to do the best with what you've got.* You may not be totally comfortable on stage yet. You may have trouble singing while playing your instrument. You may not be able to play your instrument without watching your fingers. You may not have the resources to do the types of things you'd like to do.

Over time, you will become more at ease on stage. You will become a better player, and you will learn to command the attention of the crowd. You will have the resources to amp up your production. You *will* have to put in the time to get there, however.

For the purposes of this how-to guide, I'm going to slot everything under three categories: **Preparation**, **Promotion**, and **Performance**. This would be an exhaustive subject if I was to go into every detail, but instead I've summarized the key points. I would suggest viewing these tips in context of this entire chapter.

Preparation

Frankly, when it comes to performance, there's nothing as important as the preparation stage. If you want to get the most out of your live shows, this is where you should be spending the majority of your time. A lot of musicians tend to think that a great concert is all about the performance, when in reality it's about the experience you create for your audience. Even if you think certain things are cheesy or unimportant, if they make your fans feel good, you shouldn't be too quick to write them off.

1) **Rehearse:** of course, there are very few bands that don't actually rehearse before a show; unless they know their material forwards and backwards. However, don't just play music in your rehearsals. Practice your stage moves, and plan out how each member is going to move and when. Invest in live music production materials and understand how you can make each song *look* different and not just *sound* different.

2) **Select a venue:** venue selection is more important than you might think. As a musician, you might be tempted to take gigs in every dark and dingy bar. You may be tempted to play all of the highest paying gigs. I'm not saying that you shouldn't. However, when you see things from the perspective of your fans, this simply won't do. If you want to create the greatest experience possible, you should be thinking about everything from parking space to menu items to how accessible a venue is.

3) **Get familiar with the venue:** take some time to get familiar with the venue, the stage and their equipment. Make note of the venue capacity. Make note of any extra gear you might need. See if they have a sound system and a sound tech, and if not, what solutions might be available to you. Find out if the sound tech is any good. Begin to envision how you are going to set up on stage. If possible, visit the venue when another band is playing and make notes.

4) **Sound check:** show up to the venue early and sound check before the show. Ask the event coordinator, venue owner or the sound person when would be the best time to come in. The sound tech can either be your best friend or your worst enemy depending on how you treat them. Be willing to work with them; if they are any good at what they do, "Your guitar is too loud" is usually more than just an opinion.

5) **Prepare stage props, lighting, etc.:** if you have stage props (like a vinyl sign with your band name and web address on it), lighting equipment, or video equipment, make sure to prepare these things in advance. Don't wait for the last minute to see if everything will work out. Make sure to test your gear and get it ready for your performance.

6) **Prepare your gear:** make sure that all of your music gear is in working order. If you think you might need extra strings, batteries, sticks, tuners and so forth, ensure that you have a backup supply on hand. You don't want to show up to the venue with gear that isn't going to last you the night.

7) **Prepare print materials:** depending on how you intend to promote the show, you may want to have posters, flyers, business cards, invites and/or post cards on the ready. Make sure to plan to have these materials in your hands long before your show.

Promotion

The promotion stage is where you get the word out about your show. There are a myriad of ways to do this, and if we were to broach the subject of guerrilla marketing, there would be virtually no end to the number of ways you could raise awareness of your show. Use these tips as a starting point and continue to expand your marketing efforts as you are able.

1) **Send out invites:** if you've prepared postal invites, you'll want to start sending them out at least four weeks

before the show. Make sure to create a list of people that you intend to invite, so you don't end up missing someone. Conversely, you don't want to send an invite to someone that is going to cause trouble or disrupt the performance. Use your discretion.

2) **Send out emails:** hopefully you've started collecting email addresses already. A mailing list will prove vital to your long-term success as a band, and it's a great way to promote upcoming releases and performances. Send your fans an email campaign well in advance of your next show, and don't be afraid to follow up once or twice. Nobody likes too many emails, but most people like reminders.

3) **Post to your social channels:** it's generally a good idea to let your social followers know about your upcoming show. However, if all you ever post is "Buy our album" or "Come to our show" or "Vote for us", don't expect to get much traction with your messages. Get into the habit of engaging and adding value often, and *then* let your followers know what they can do for you.

4) **Hand out your flyers**: flyers aren't necessarily the most effective way to promote your shows. Some see it as a way to raise awareness of their show, and if not, their music. That may be true, but I would suggest targeting your audience to the best of your ability. It's pretty much a roll of the dice whether or not someone on the street is going to like your show or actually come to it, but you can guess with some accuracy whether or not

music students, weekend partiers, and venue regulars are going to be interested, just as an example. Another way to increase the effectiveness of your flyers is to create a promotion around it. For example, you could give an album away to the person who brings the flyer with them, or let them in to the venue free of charge.

5) **Post your posters:** like flyers, posters may not have a dramatic effect on your live show attendance. There tend to be a lot of people competing for the same space, be it community bulletin boards or poster poles. If you go out of your way, you *will* find boards that don't have a lot of other postings on them. However, if there aren't any posters there, you also have to wonder how often people actually look in those places. I am not saying that posters can't be of some use; they tend to be fairly effective for well-known acts. The main thing to remember here is to look for creative ways to stand out from your competition, whether it's with a unique design or enticing offers.

6) **Send out texts:** if you've implemented a text messaging service on your website and some fans have opted in to receive messages from you (whenever you have a show), don't forget to send them a message letting them know about your performance.

7) **Make phone calls:** oftentimes, the most effective way of getting your fans out to a live show is personal contact. You may not have the time or resources to call all of your fans, but if you've been playing for a while,

you should be able to identify your key fans. Put a priority on calling those people.

Performance

Finally, the day of the show has arrived. Now it's time to get on stage and play. However, don't forget that you are there for the fans and not the other way around. Your job is done when you've followed up with the leads you've generated from the show, possibly even a week later; not when you've played the last note to the last song.

1) **Play the show:** naturally, when the time comes, you have to deliver on your promises. I have seen a lot of bands wait around to see if more people show up before going onstage. Don't do this unless the coordinator or booker suggests that you do. There will always be fans who say, "Oh man, I can't believe I only caught the last five songs of your set!" Believe me; I've seen it many times. It's not a bad way to leave them wanting more. Invite them out to your next show.

2) **Entertain and engage the audience:** ultimately, the show is about the fans and how you make them feel. Playing music is fun, and that's as it should be. However, don't forget who you're playing for. Get your fans involved as much as you can; but don't patronize if at all possible.

3) **Meet your fans:** the show isn't over when you finish playing the last note. The show is over when your fans go home. You need to shake hands, sign autographs,

and include everyone you see (yes, even those who are standing off to the side). Some venues will be more lenient about meet & greets after the show than others, so try to remain sensitive to their business hours and staff as well. Take it outside (or to another place) if you have to.

4) **Write 'Thank You' notes:** this is a small thing, but it can go a long way. If you prefer, you can have 'Thank You' notes pre-signed and ready to be handed out before you ever get to the venue. Either way, let the key people know how appreciated they are.

5) **Follow up:** whether you had a bad show or a great show, don't forget to follow up with your fans. If it wasn't so good, talk about the good points. If it was great, talk about the good points. Either way, talk about the good points! This is a good way to stay in the consciousness of your fans. In addition, there may have been people that wanted to buy your merch or check out your website, but for whatever reason, haven't yet. The profitability of a show doesn't need to end the moment you leave the venue. You can cast a wider net later, and snag a few more sales, subscribers or followers if you're shrewd.

Conclusion

Performing live can be a lot of fun, and it should be. However, never forget that an effective live show will translate into making more money and generating more opportunities. In other words, if you aren't gaining any traction with your live shows, it could be due to inexperience, but it could also be due to a lack of planning.

If you haven't watched a mainstream live performance from the likes of Beyoncé or Marianas Trench in a while, I would encourage you to go and watch one on YouTube now and observe it very carefully. What you discover may surprise you; **professional shows are usually planned out to the last detail**! Even little moves and flourishes that might seem "improvised" have generally been practiced.

This is, perhaps, one of the best-kept secrets of the industry. A lot of independent musicians are often too stubborn to consider whether or not their stage presence is actually connecting with the audience. They feel like they should be able to get the same results as the pros by "winging it".

If you like to wing it, that's totally fine. Again, you should know your own goals better than anyone else. However, if you want your performances to leave a lasting impression, don't leave too many details to chance.

What I Like

I enjoy live performance in general. Performing as a 15-year-old left such a lasting impression on me that I ended up dedicating a large part of the subsequent 13 to 14 years of my life pursuing a career in music.

From hot dog lunches to networking events, I've performed in a variety of settings. Even so, I have to say that nothing matches the excitement and fun of performing on a *real* stage with a *real* band.

What I Don't Like

I didn't like playing to small, non-existent or non-responsive audiences. I thought that my career should have been moving forward with every show I played, and when it didn't pay off or present any new opportunities, I would get discouraged.

To be honest, that might be the difference between the pros and I. I did try to make the most of shows where the audience was not feeding back the energy I was sending out, but sometimes it got on my nerves. I think the pros know that a price has to be paid, and they have a long-term perspective that allows them to see these shows as stepping blocks, however small.

I did not realize this until much later in my career, but when I did, I was able to keep a better attitude around empty venues.

Action Steps

➢ **Decide:** you may not be ready to decide on a career path yet, and that's okay. There may be information in the following chapters that enables you to make a more informed decision. However, at some point, you will need to choose whether live performance should be a part of your plan or not.

➢ **Define your roles:** take some time to divvy up tasks between your band members and/or your team. If you don't have band members or a team, simply start creating a list of the different items that need to be done on a daily, weekly, monthly and yearly basis. If you're in a band, each member should be contributing to the forward momentum of it. Make sure everyone knows what they are supposed to be doing. If you're alone right now, start making task lists. You *want* to have a team one day, right?

➤ **Keep a list of venues and contacts:** always keep track of venues you've played in, and make note of venues that you haven't played in yet. Add to your list as you find more. Create three categories: local, at a distance, and long distance. Local venues, of course, would be those in your hometown. At a distance would be venues within a three hour radius of where you live. Though it may sound tiring, you can make your way out to these venues - even on a weeknight - perform, and return home in time for a bit of rest. Long distance venues would be those that are outside of a three hour radius. These are towns you might have to fly to or travel to on tour. Also make a list of the people you come in contact with and create a database of their information.

➤ **Create your checklists:** don't forget to create your performance, marketing and music gear checklists. These tools will prove invaluable, and they will help you to make the most of each and every concert.

8. Radio

 TV gives everyone an image, but radio gives birth to a million images in a million brains. - Peggy Nooma

Up until recently, I had mistakenly thought that radio was a dying medium, along with newspapers, CDs, and books. As it turns out, there's still a market for all of those things. Cloud based storage and low-cost services have meant that the need to own digital media is mostly non-existent. However, there is still a large demographic of people who prefer to own physical product, for the experience, for the tactility, or for the sake of familiarity.

Radio is very much alive, and it can still be used to generate significant exposure for one's music. It has certain advantages over most other promotional tools, because it's possible to get immediate and widespread attention.

That type of exposure is not a guarantee by any means, but radio still seems to fill a niche that hasn't totally been replaced yet; even with the emergence of internet radio and podcasts. It may surprise you to know that radio is still the top overall music discovery tool, even with the growing popularity of streaming sites and YouTube.

Radio can benefit your career in meaningful ways if you know how to leverage it.

Introduction to Radio

Certainly, getting your music played on radio is one way to leverage the medium. However, you should be aware that there are several other ways of marketing your music with the platform.

For example, you could schedule interviews. You could offer to play acoustic versions of your songs on air. You could guest host. You could record bumpers. You may even be able to do all of these things at once.

Not all stations or DJs will be open to these ideas, but even **radio promotion tours** aren't completely unheard of, so with adequate planning and research, it is likely that you could get a foot in the door this way.

It is also possible to supplement your touring activities by setting up radio engagements. A lot of smaller, community oriented radio stations might even be okay with you dropping in to say "hi".

In fact, this is exactly what we did on both of Jonathan Ferguson's British Columbia tours. At our first visit to Creston, BC, we dropped in at Creston Community Radio CIDO 97.7 FM. We built connections with the volunteers rather quickly, and before we knew it we were asked to come in and play a few songs, on air, to promote our upcoming show at the Snoring Sasquatch. When we returned to Creston the following year, they had us in to do another interview and we played a few acoustic numbers on that occasion as well.

The people in Creston are quite friendly, so this may sound altogether too easy. However, I could see it working with other community minded radio stations. Just remember to keep an eye out for these types of opportunities, especially while you are on the road.

Community or university and college radio stations may not be able to offer you the type of exposure that commercial radio could, but it can still be quite helpful in promoting local performances.

DJs are Expert Marketers

I'm pretty sure this statement came straight from the mouth of a radio DJ, so take it with some bias, but radio DJs tend to do a great job of promoting everything from local events, products, to businesses and of course, music. It seems logical, since radio is a medium that has been around for a long time, has a proven track record, and has successfully marketed many items in the past. DJs have had time to develop their taste-making skills. That would be one reason to pursue radio promotion and airplay.

Another reason to pursue airplay is for the possible earnings you can generate if you are a SOCAN, ASCAP or BMI member. You may not earn a significant amount of money at first, but when you're pursuing a career in music, every stream of income counts.

Perhaps you've heard the story of how Collective Soul finally broke through. Singer Ed Roland was an active musician in Atlanta since the mid-1980s. However, over time, many of his music collaborations fell through, so he enlisted the help of a few musicians to record a demo in his basement. Roland recorded the songs with the intention of selling them to a publishing company. However, his demo was passed along to WJRR in Orlando, which started playing "Shine", and it quickly became the most requested song on that station. That's the power of radio. If not for that incident, Collective Soul may not be where they are today.

You *want* to get radio DJs on your side. Unfortunately, commercial radio is progressively taking over the airwaves, which has meant fewer opportunities for independent artists. Having said that, you just never know what doors your connections could open for you.

The Different Types of Radio

There are basically five different types of radio, and if you want to tap into the world of radio promotion, it is crucial that you understand each of them.

Commercial radio is owned by large media conglomerates and is the most popular, most widely listened-to format. Sadly, based on my research, getting played on commercial radio as an independent artist is an uphill battle, except on specialty programs. If you want to put out feelers with your radio campaigns anyway (I certainly did), you could give it a shot, but it's not very likely to yield the kind of results you're looking for.

Other than commercial radio, there's **college & non-profit**, **community**, **internet radio & podcasts**, as well as **satellite radio**. Fortunately, there are many opportunities available for independent musicians in all of these formats. It would be a good idea to make these stations a greater priority with your campaigns.

Let's take a look at each of these formats in a little more detail.

- **Commercial radio:** the main goal of commercial radio is to sell advertising and commercials, as this is what helps them to meet their operating budget. Non-commercial radio, by contrast, is not usually concerned with other avenues of revenue. Therefore, ratings are of primary importance to commercial radio stations, as the fees that can be collected from advertisers are generally in proportion to their ratings. That might explain why their playlists are dominated by familiar top 40 songs that appeal to the masses. New artists are generally passed up for the simple reason that they do not have enough clout or notoriety to keep listener interest. New artists that are backed by a big budget may be the rare exception. Commercial radio stations generally work with labels and promoters to help them decide on their playlist, and give considerable weight to factors like consumer availability (in-store, online, etc.), publicity, performance and appearances (especially local), advertising, and visibility in media campaigns, to determine what songs will be a part of their programming. In other words, the potential exposure of a song is instrumental in whether or not a commercial station chooses to play it. As an independent artist, you may get played on a specialty program. However, that's usually an indicator that you do *not* fit their format; it's not a precursor to being played on their primary programming.

- **College & non-profit radio:** campus or college radio is usually student-driven. College, university or other educational institutions serve as the home to these stations. Programming is typically organized by the students, the community at large, or a combination thereof. Some campus radio stations exist for the purpose of training future radio professionals, while others exist to provide an alternative to commercial or governmental broadcasters. The format is a little more free-form compared to commercial radio, with a mix of news, sports, spoken word and a variety of different styles of emerging and trending music.

- **Community radio:** community radio stations generally serve their immediate locality and they are often non-profit. Their content and programming is dictated by a specific local audience. It enables individuals, groups and communities to voice their own opinions and tell their own stories, and become contributors to the media at large. On community radio, you will probably hear content that is unique to their programming, especially in contrast to commercial radio. Specialized music shows can often be heard on community stations as well.

- **Internet radio & podcasts:** internet radio, naturally, is a type of radio that is transmitted over the internet. Internet radio utilizes streaming media, which means that broadcasts usually can't be paused or replayed. Broadcasters offer news, sports, talk and music; formats that can be found on most traditional terrestrial stations. Some internet stations are associated with larger traditional stations, but independent stations have also grown in number thanks to low operation costs. Podcasts, on the other hand, can be subscribed to and downloaded through syndication platforms like iTunes. They can also be streamed online on a variety of devices. Podcasts can be played, paused and replayed, unlike internet radio programming. Though audio is the most popular format, video, PDF and ePub files can also be distributed through podcasts.

- **Satellite radio:** satellite radio is primarily a broadcast service for in-car listening. Signals are broadcast nationwide, allowing them to reach larger geographical areas than terrestrial radio. Satellite radio is a subscription based service that is mostly commercial free, and subscribers can access a wider variety of programming options than with traditional radio.

Radio Campaigns

The most accessible and practical way of getting airplay as an independent artist is with the College market. CD Baby and Derek Sivers have already covered this topic extremely well, so I will summarize their main points here. What follows may not be the definitive guide, but based on my research, it is some of the best information available.

Here's how to put together a College radio campaign:

1) Determine the number of mailings you want to send out. Anywhere from 100 to 500 packages seems to be common. Make sure to create a budget for the mail-outs.

2) Send out one CD per station and make sure the cellophane wrapper is removed (and yes, *do* send them a professionally pressed **CD** and *not* an mp3 or a burned disc unless they request it). The little things will make a difference in the success of your campaign, so don't forget to practice professionalism.

3) Include your band's one-sheet with the name of your band, contact information, URLs, band photo, album art, track listing, and a bio. Highlight the songs in your track list that you want the DJs to listen to.

4) Make a list of the stations and programs you're going to mail your packages to. This list should ideally be made up of places you can realistically tour through three to four times per year.

5) Address your packages to radio programmers and DJs by name. Do not address them to "dear sir/madam" unless you absolutely have to.

6) Follow up with each station by phone or email in two week's time.

7) Ask if the station received your package, if they've listened to your music, and whether or not they are considering it for airplay.

8) Remember to keep communication succinct. If the station is not considering your music for their programming, you *can* ask why, but otherwise just say "thank you" and move on. Don't push the issue, don't negotiate, and don't get defensive.

9) Check back every few weeks with the stations that have decided to play your music to continue to get played and develop relationships with the radio programmers. It couldn't hurt to build relationships with the stations that choose not to play your music either.

Internet radio, satellite radio and podcasts have their own unique submission guidelines, so make sure to observe their conduct rules for best results. Their guidelines usually appear on their websites.

If you are looking for podcasts to submit your music to, you can search iTunes. As you are looking for shows to submit your music to, remember to search for podcasts that already have an independent focus and play the style of music you create.

If you are looking for internet radio stations, search on sites like Live365 or SHOUTcast. Again, always look for shows that cater to your specific genre or style of music.

Finally, remember to be tactful in your interactions. Always present yourself professionally. See if you can provide added value to the program directors you come in contact with (i.e. contests and/or promotions).

My Experience

My experience with radio is not extensive, but I thought I would share what I've found with you.

I recall initiating one small campaign (maybe 20 to 30 packages) after releasing my first solo album in 2006, which, surprisingly, got me some airplay within the province of Alberta, Canada. My first CD certainly wasn't my best, but fortunately I was able to appeal to the college market with it. This showed me that it is definitely possible to earn radio airplay, though you should take some time to research the stations you're sending your music to. It seems like common sense, but as much as possible, you should send your packages to programs that your music actually fits.

I remember writing up handwritten notes (with a Sharpie marker) for each station I sent a package to. That way, my packages would always have a personal touch, and radio stations would know right away that they weren't just getting a form letter or an unsolicited package. I'm not sure how effective this was, but ultimately, I don't think it hurt me any.

Another thing I'd like to point out is that radio campaigns take a bit of determination and perseverance. In our day-to-day lives, it's too easy to get distracted and forget to follow up. I have heard it said before that follow-up is the most important part of developing a relationship with prospects, and I think that to be the case with radio. It's not your job to be a pest, but you'll definitely want to follow up and (in some cases) keep in touch with the stations you contact. Otherwise, your package will have been in vain, because the stations will assume that you just don't care. If you truly believe in your music, show them how strong your belief is.

How to Promote Your Music with Radio

The basic formula for radio promotion was essentially outlined in the **Radio Campaigns** section. This how-to guide elaborates on these points in a little more detail.

You should be aware that though you can initiate and handle all of the campaign duties on your own - and that will likely be the cheapest way - there are also radio promotion companies like Bryan Farrish Marketing that can help you organize your promotional campaigns. By all accounts, I have heard that they are good at what they do, but their services do cost money.

The Do It Yourself (DIY) route may seem like the best way, though undoubtedly it will require more of your time and effort. You may have to make decisions based on budgetary constraints at first, but once the income starts flowing, you may want to consider enlisting the help of others. In the long run, you can accomplish a lot more when you have a team that is willing to help you.

Here's how to promote your music with radio:

1) **Define your goals:** whatever it is you want to accomplish with a radio promotion, make sure to start with an end goal in mind. Haphazardly sending out your music to hundreds of stations simply because you have a new album isn't going to take you very far. Moreover, it's going to end up costing you both time and money that could have been spent elsewhere. If you want radio promotion to complement your touring efforts, send your music to towns and cities that you know you're

going to be performing at. If you play a specific genre of music, look for programs that actually play your style of music. Get specific.

2) **Make a list of radio stations:** make a list of the stations that you're going to be sending your packages to. Don't mark down every station that you find. Just keep track of the ones that play your style of music. Keep detailed contact information for each, as you will need to follow up with them later. Keep this list for posterity, as you can always use it again for future campaigns. Also remember to target non-commercial stations primarily, unless you want to put a few feelers out with commercial radio.

3) **Plan:** decide how many packages you're going to be sending out, and create a budget for your campaign. Figure out whether or not you want to send out all of the packages at the same time. If so, keep in mind that you will have to make all of your follow-up calls in one sitting as well. If you're going to stagger your mail-outs, make sure to keep meticulous notes, as you need to contact stations in a timely manner; not too early (before the CD arrives), and not too late (after the package has been thrown into the trash bin). Leave a two-week buffer before getting in touch.

4) **Prepare your packages:** include an unwrapped CD and a one-sheet (with your band photo, album artwork, bio, contact information, relevant links and highlighted tracks) in your campaign packages. Make sure to

address your envelopes to a person, and not to a station. Don't forget; even envelopes can be customized. You do not have to send out your packages in generic white or orange bubble mailers if you're eager to stand out. You will likely need a budget to have custom-made envelopes printed, but it is a great way to get the attention of radio stations and DJs. How you approach radio promotion also depends on the aesthetic of your band and your music. For example, if you're in a death metal band, a bloodied looking envelope could prove interesting (but not *real* blood please). Additionally, you could include a few smaller freebies in your mailer; stickers, buttons, postcards, etc. It is certainly not a requirement, and some stations will probably toss them out, but some will appreciate them.

5) **Send out your packages:** once all of your packages are ready, it's time to send them out. If you haven't decided whether you're going to send them all at once or stagger their mail-out date, make sure to decide now. Again, if you have 500 mailings or more, you're going to have a lot of follow-up work to do on the back end, so keep things simple. If you want to spread out the work a bit, then stagger your mailings.

6) **Follow up:** after two weeks, remember to follow up with every radio station you've sent a package to. You can contact them by phone or email, but if they specifically mentioned their preferred contact method on their website, make sure to observe that. Don't call people who want to be emailed, and don't email people

who want to be called. Once you get a hold of them, simply ask whether or not they are considering your music for airplay, and if not, you should end the conversation quickly. You *can* ask why they're not interested in your music, but remember not to push the issue too much. Even if a particular station isn't interested in playing your music, you don't have to cross them off of your list. You can try again with your next release, assuming they actually play your style of music and you fit their format.

7) **Stay in touch:** you can continue to build relationships with the stations and DJs that have chosen to play your music on air. This is a good thing to do, because you will keep top-of-mind with the influencers and tastemakers of the industry. New opportunities might come your way. Even if not for that, you will continue to get played long after other artists that lost interest in maintaining relationships with the DJs.

>> Tools & Tips

To access these and other resources, go to: **http://dawcast.com/the-new-music-industry-resource-list/**

> ➤ **Radio Promotion 101:** if you'd like to go deeper into the world of radio promotion, I would recommend checking out what the experts have

had to say on the subject. By accessing this resource, you can read dozen or so articles written by Bryan Farrish, who is certainly qualified to speak on the topic of radio.

Conclusion

In coming years, it is possible that sites like YouTube or Pandora may take over as the primary music discovery tools. Until then, radio is still the best way to get your music heard by a larger audience and to get exposure for it.

The challenge, of course, is in getting played on stations that people actually listen to. With commercial radio out of the picture, this can be a more challenging feat than it sounds.

Then, your music has to be good enough for people to want to hear it *again*. People have to hear something to like it, and then they have to like it to want to buy it. This is the Hear / Like / Buy formula that Andrew Dubber talked about in his e-book, *The 20 Things You Must Know About Music Online*. This blueprint is crucial to understand, especially as it pertains to radio airplay and, by extension, any other public placement (the mall, retail stores, etc.).

In other words, the immediate benefit of radio airplay may not necessarily be more album sales, though that is one of the implications. There are always other benefits, be it building awareness for your music or residual earnings from being played on the radio.

One of the downsides of video sharing sites is that if a site like YouTube does become a more ubiquitous music discovery platform, it may become even harder for artists to get immediate and widespread exposure for their music like they have been with radio. An unbelievable number of videos are uploaded to YouTube every single day, and only a percentage of them ever become popular.

However, my gut feeling - based on where things have been going - is that the continued growth of streaming sites and other music discovery platforms is going to scatter listeners across many different channels. Let's hope that distribution keeps up with demand.

Fundamentally, you don't *have* to use radio to promote your music. Depending on your goals and what career path you intend to take, it may not be important to you. Only you can make that decision.

What I Like

➢ **Interviews:** having been on the radio a couple of times, I must say that in-studio interviews and performances are a lot of fun. If you've never done it before, I would definitely recommend finding community radio stations in your area that are interested in having you on. In my experience, some are even willing to fly by the seat of their pants, so you could try dropping in unannounced. Don't forget to be courteous and professional, however.

➢ **Airplay:** there is definitely something special about having your song played on the radio. I can't say that I've ever been listening to the radio at the exact moment my song was on-air, but even just a note from a DJ letting you know that they are using your song in their programming is a cool feeling. It's even cooler when your song starts to connect with people.

➢ **Podcasts:** I have dedicated an entire chapter to the subject of podcasting in this guide already, so there isn't too much to say here. The great thing about podcasting is that not only can you licence your music to be played on other podcasts, you can also create your own show to promote your music and your career activities. It's a powerful medium with a lot of potential for willing musicians.

➢ **Internet radio:** my music listening habits have changed considerably over time. I can remember listening to cassette tapes as a kid. Then CDs came out. Then Napster came along. Then music became all the more accessible on the internet. These days, I find myself listening to various electronic mixes on YouTube (as I work), but I can also remember a time when I listened to internet radio quite a bit. I still think it's a pretty cool medium, since you can find a lot of variety and specialty programming.

➢ **SomaFM:** speaking of internet radio and streaming, this is probably my go-to place. SomaFM offers 20 channels of commercial free, listener-supported underground and alternative radio from San Francisco. All of the music they play is handpicked by their award-winning music directors and DJs. My favourite channel is Groove Salad, which features ambient and downtempo beats and grooves. It's great for working and chilling out.

➢ **Fiverr:** Fiverr is a marketplace where providers offer a variety of different services for only $5. There is virtually no end to the ways in which a musician could take advantage of this platform to promote their music, and radio promotion is no exception. From people that will air your song on the radio to those who will play your ad on their show, you can find a variety of interesting offers on the site. Though you will likely want to do some research before paying for anyone's services, at the low cost of $5, you're bound to find some winning propositions. Even if some aren't, you could do a lot worse.

To access these and other resources, go to: **http://dawcast.com/the-new-music-industry-resource-list/**

What I Don't Like

➢ **Marketing messages:** sometimes you just don't know how you got onto someone's mailing list. While I was still actively pursuing a career in music, I can remember getting regular email messages from radio promotion companies, and it really annoyed me after a while. In fact, I think I still get messages like that. Radio campaigns can be really expensive if you go through a promotion company to do it, and I simply didn't have the budget to work with them at the time. That didn't stop them from emailing me and calling me. However, I am certainly not advocating that you avoid these companies. They might actually be able to provide you with new opportunities. Just keep in mind that their campaigns aren't likely to be that much different from what you could do on your own. It's not like radio stations are hard to find. A promotion company could help you save some time, and maybe even help you target stations you couldn't reach otherwise, but you will spend a pretty penny for it.

> **Commercial radio:** it's not that I dislike commercial radio because they don't play independent musicians, although that may be part of it. I can remember a time, especially in the late 90s, when mainstream radio was still good, or *at least* decent. Top 40 music was tolerable, and sometimes it was even really good. However, that's not really the case anymore. The lyrical content found in modern hits is atrocious; even if the beat or the groove is catchy, the overall message of the song is anything but meaningful, intelligent or subtle.

Action Steps

Now you know the different types of radio and how to orchestrate a radio campaign. When you are ready to act on the information provided here, remember to review this section.

> **Decide:** how important is radio promotion to you? Some careers in music are built on radio, while others

100

are not. Some are built with a combination of different mediums. Any way you look at it, success in music is going to take hard work and effort. Radio may offer some advantages, but it may have some downsides too. If you are excited about the prospect of being on the radio, then it's a career choice that probably makes sense to you. If it doesn't get you fired up, it's entirely possible that you won't need the medium to make your dreams a reality. Moreover, independent artists can't do everything; especially when they are first getting started. Radio might be something you grow into.

- ➤ **Understand the different types of radio:** if radio promotion is something you want to explore further, make sure that you understand the different types of radio that were explained in this chapter. Your radio campaigns will be less effective if you approach them haphazardly. There has to be some planning and goal-setting behind your efforts. Though you can always put some feelers out, targeting commercial radio stations isn't likely to be terribly worthwhile. You will have to find your opportunities in non-commercial radio. When you know the ins and outs of radio, you can make the most of your campaigns, which, by the way, do cost money. Make sure to create a budget for said campaigns.

- ➤ **Understand the different types of opportunities:** airplay is just one facet of radio promotion. Keep in mind that there is more to radio than just getting your song played. You can advertise. You can schedule interviews. You can book in-studio performances. You might even be able to organize promotions and giveaways, co-host or record bumpers for the station. Remember to develop relationships with the DJs to find out if they would be interested in working on a promotion together. You want these people on your side.

➢ **Plan and organize your campaigns:** if you're going to mail out hundreds of packages to radio stations everywhere, you might as well make it worth your while. Follow up with each station that you send your package to and plan to tour through the towns and cities where the stations are located.

9. Music Instruction

 We know an age more vividly through its music than through its historians. - Rosanne Ambrose-Brown

Thinking about becoming a music teacher? It's a respectable profession with decent pay, rewards, flexible hours, and can generate additional paying opportunities (it has for me) like show bookings, workshops, recitals and more. It can also be used as a vehicle to create a supplemental income stream (just look at Tom Hess).

I have been teaching music for over 10 years, and though I have found that it requires a lot of energy, it has grown into a significant source of income for me, from teaching in studios to workshops to private lessons.

If you choose to get into teaching, it's important to recognize that you need to become more others-focused. When you're busy learning other artist's material, you probably won't have as much time to work on your own music as you would like, but you can still learn a lot and grow a lot as a musician in the process.

I have heard that a six-figure income is possible in music instruction, and I don't really doubt it. I have never earned that much in a year myself, but if it sounds appealing to you, I've done my best to explain how you can become a highly paid teacher in this chapter.

Introduction to Music Instruction

One of the amazing things about music instruction is that it will shed light on your weaknesses as a musician and instrumentalist. I say that it's "Amazing", because, your students will make you aware of areas where you're not as strong as you would like to be or thought you were. You will also realize that there are a great many things you do automatically, without fully understanding how it works technically or theoretically. As a teacher, you will have to learn to analyze and deconstruct your playing.

If you want to be a teacher, be prepared to go deeper into rudiments and theory, because if you don't know how to explain basic concepts, you will have to *learn* how. If you don't know certain songs, you may have to study them. You may even have to learn intros and riffs without ever learning full songs. This is just part of the job description; some songs, exercises and riffs will serve the purposes of your lessons, while others won't.

Some people may later criticize your ability to play many intros without being able to play "full songs". Some people value that more than having a diverse repertoire, and certainly if your students make it their goal to learn entire songs, you should help them do that. However, this can't be forced. Don't concern yourself too much with what others think, because how you learn, grow and progress will look decidedly different than anyone else.

Ideally, you'll want to become a player that knows their instrument inside and out. If you are a guitarist, for example, you should know all of the notes on the fretboard, understand chord construction, and know how scales work and how to apply them; not just how to play them.

Fortunately, there are a lot of online lessons and resources that you can take advantage of, and many of them are free. You can find a rather large catalogue of lessons on YouTube, just as an example. Whether you want to learn scales or songs, chances are pretty good that someone has created a lesson around it.

>> Tools & Tips for Guitarists

To access these and other resources, go to:
http://dawcast.com/the-new-music-industry-resource-list/

> **Ultimate Guitar:** Ultimate Guitar features a large archive of guitar tabs, lessons and articles. Though you should never put yourself in a position where you are relying on guitar tabs alone (it's better to learn the fretboard and develop your ear), you can certainly leverage the resources there to augment your knowledge and playing. Most of their offerings are entirely free.

> **Power Tab:** if you are going to use Ultimate

Guitar, I would recommend downloading Power Tab as well. If you search for a song on Ultimate Guitar, you will notice that some of them are marked 'power tab' on the side. You cannot download and view these files unless you have the Power Tab software, which is a tablature authoring tool for Windows. Many people like to use this tool to create tabs, as it allows them to view tablature and standard notation for their music simultaneously. In addition, you can playback and listen to the tab (with MIDI instruments), you can slow down or speed up the tempo of the song, and you can even change the tuning of the guitars as necessary. This is a great learning tool, but it can also be used to create original compositions as well. The tracks you create can be exported to MIDI, which means you can compose in Power Tab, export to MIDI, bring it into your favourite DAW, and add some flourish to your recordings by assigning VST plugins to the MIDI tracks you created. This works well for people who know music well enough to compose but can't play every instrument under the sun.

➤ **Guitar Pro:** the Guitar Pro software is fairly similar to Power Tab, but it's more feature-rich. As such, it also costs a bit of money. Again, some of the tab files you'll find on a site like Ultimate

Guitar will be marked 'guitar pro', and you cannot view or use these files unless you have the program. Personally, I like to use both Power Tab *and* Guitar Pro. You will find that some tab interpretations are better than others, so if you want to be able to access the best transcriptions of your favourite songs, you may end up needing both programs. As far as sound goes, Guitar Pro far exceeds what Power Tab is capable of.

The Different Types of Music Instruction

I should point out that there are a few different paths for music instructors. In a broader sense, there's private instruction, in-store instruction, and institutional instruction (schools, conservatories, etc.).

Each of these paths is a little different, though you may find yourself mixing and matching at times. I've provided a brief description for each of these paths below.

Private instruction is where you develop your own client base and teach them, or you go through an in-home lesson agency that provides clients to you. You may find it necessary to use both methods to flesh out your schedule.

When it comes to your own clients, you have considerable freedom. You can have them come to your studio, or you can go to their home to teach them there. You can set your own rates and your own hours too.

Many classical piano and violin teachers tend to teach from their homes. However, depending on your competition, you may find it difficult to get your students to come directly to you. If there is someone out there offering a more convenient and affordable service than you are, you will have to find a way to compete.

If you are an established or reputable teacher, the game changes dramatically. You would have even more control over your rates, your terms, and students will be more willing to come to your home for lessons.

Notwithstanding, you will have to build up to that point. You could have a decade of experience behind you and still not be a recognized instructor. It all depends on how you position yourself.

You will have to approach your career holistically. In my experience, you can't build a reputation merely by being a great musician or a great teacher. You have to be a great *person* too. There is a meaningful balance.

In my experience, teachers are often required to play the part of the mentor, motivational speaker, coach, and even psychologist. Naturally, you can't take on other people's problems as your own, but you do have to get your students into the right state of mind to learn. Sometimes this might require a little bit of encouragement.

In-store instruction is where you go to a local music store and teach lessons in their in-store lesson facilities. Teachers are generally self-employed, even in this context. Personally, even while teaching in stores, I would often maintain a private client base outside of my hours at a particular store. In some cases, this may be frowned upon, but unless they are helping you to get a reasonable client base in-store, their concerns are essentially moot. They have to be willing to fill up your schedule if they expect you to drop outside activities.

With that in mind, it is certainly possible to build up your schedule to the point where you are teaching five to six days a week (roughly 30 to 40 hours a week, depending on your availability and the availability of your students). Teaching hours are generally evenings and weekends, but you may find some students who are willing to come in earlier in the day or even in the morning.

Most stores book lessons in 30 minute intervals, so keep in mind that if you are working 30 to 40 hours a week, you would be teaching anywhere from 60 to 70 students! That's a lot of people to keep track of.

Notwithstanding, you will likely be paid a little less in stores than you could be earning privately. It's a bit of a trade-off, because music stores will usually manage your schedule on your behalf. They also have a built-in client base because of their storefront, an advertising infrastructure and publicity that enables them to build their brand recognition. You also don't have to drive around to different locations to teach. You can stay put in one spot.

You don't necessarily require any formal education to pursue in-store or even private instruction. You should have *some* musical training behind you, however.

If you do have formal training, then you may be able to earn more money from the get-go. Of course, not all private or in-store teachers have educational credentials

One of the major drawbacks of in-store instruction is that there is usually very little guidance or feedback on behalf of the employer. What this means is that, you could be the nicest person in the world, but if a student doesn't like you for any reason at all and they tell the store staff, you could be "flagged" and up for evaluation.

While I have found that most employers will express understanding and cross these bridges as they come to them, the greater loss is usually self-confidence. These incidents will rarely lead to the loss of a job, unless they compound.

Unfortunately, no matter how good of a person or teacher you are, some people just won't like you. I encountered these situations several times over the course of 10 years, and while it may have been justified in some circumstances, the majority of cases were essentially anomalies. A student would begin to build a "case" for why they thought I wasn't very good at what I did. Usually, their concerns were not based in any permutation of reality.

Institutional instruction is where you study to become a qualified music teacher for elementary school, secondary school, college, university or a conservatory. For elementary or secondary school, you will require a Bachelors Degree in Music Education, and if you want to teach at the higher levels, you will need an advanced degree, such as a Master's Degree in Music Education.

Elementary and secondary school teachers have set hours and established policies that must be followed. A music teacher in this capacity may also have non-teaching duties like monitoring study sessions or classes. Some rehearsals may occur on evenings or weekends as well.

At the college level, you tend to have a more flexible schedule at 12 to 16 hours a week. However, your time will also be spent preparing for lessons, rehearsing, writing, performing and attending conferences.

Income levels tend to vary considerably in this area. I don't personally have any experience with institutional instruction, but if you'd like to teach and make music for a living, it's a path worth researching in more detail.

>> Tools & Tips

To access these and other resources, go to: **http://dawcast.com/the-new-music-industry-resource-list/**

> **#028: Music Instruction with Patrick Zelinski in Calgary, AB**: Patrick Zelinski and I discuss the topic of music instruction in more detail in this

podcast episode. We cover some of the ups and downs of music instruction, as well as the work ethic that it requires.

➢ **#050: Is Substitute Music Instruction Right for You?**: I have noticed an increase in demand for substitute music instructors. In fact, I have been substituting for different teachers for about a year now, and though it can't be counted on for a full-time income, there is a steady supply of teachers that need someone to fill in. Some teachers like to get away. Others have busy gigging schedules. If you'd like to learn more about subbing, this podcast episode should steer you in the right direction.

Wages

My pay at music studios started around $7 per lesson ($14 an hour CAD) and continues to increase. Today, in most cases I earn $15 per lesson ($30 an hour).

Of course, as a music instructor, I've never been in a situation where I was working eight hours a day, five days a week. A teacher's schedule usually runs from about 4 PM to 9 PM (sometimes 3:30 PM to 9 PM) on weekdays (weekends optional).

To put it into perspective, if you were teaching at $12.50 per lesson and taught 50 students a week for a month, you would have earned about $2,500 for a month's work. 50 students would be quite a lot to take on as a teacher already, although I have heard of some teachers that teach upwards of 60 or 70 students. You could fill your weekends too if you wanted to, as there are no limitations there. If you did that, you wouldn't have as much time to rehearse or gig, as I'm sure you're beginning to see.

If you're teaching privately, it's definitely possible to charge more; anywhere from $20 - $120 or more depending on your skill level, the length of the lesson and how well you're known.

From much trial and error, I have found that you should only offer a couple of different options for lesson length. I would suggest creating 45-minute and one-hour options for your private students. 30 minute lessons are typical in music studios, but with private lessons you will probably be driving around more (you could teach from home, but unless you're a well-established teacher, it can be tough finding students that will come to you) and you'll have to account for travel time and breaks. Make the lessons worth your time and your client's time too.

The most I've made with private on-site piano lessons is $60 an hour and $50 an hour with guitar. Any more than that and I didn't seem to attract as many students. It all depends on the situation. You might be able to charge more; you might have to charge less. The prospect of earning $200 to $300 a night is definitely more appealing than teaching at a studio, but of course you have to consider the cost, time and effort in marketing yourself as a private instructor. You can't generally take on the same number of students in an evening as you could at a studio either. You also have to account for food, taxes, gas, and vehicle maintenance costs.

Another factor that can affect teaching income is the summer and Holiday seasons. Most of the time, these phases are a write-off. You will find that a large chunk of your schedule will be dictated to you by the school year, as most of your students are likely to be in grade school. Some students might stick around for summer lessons, but they are usually the minority. If nine-and-a-half months' income isn't likely to meet your needs, you'll at least want a backup plan for summer. Of course, if you only teach from 4 PM to 9 PM, you could hold a part-time job of sorts, and see if they would be willing to increase your hours over the summer.

Finally, your income is not consistent or predictable with private instruction. You will have months where you do better than others. You won't be teaching much during the winter Holidays. Some students will leave, some will stick around, and some will passionately pursue it. Some will show up to lessons, others won't.

That segues nicely into my next point...

Turnover

I have yet to experience a single teaching year where there wasn't roughly a 30 to 40% turnover rate. I'm not saying this is standard across the board, but inevitably you will have students that quit, pursue other options, or flake. You can't avoid it, so it's best to approach it with a laid-back attitude. The good news is that these holes are usually filled by new students, if not a surplus of students the following school year. Incidentally, sometimes it takes until October for your schedule to solidify.

I have also observed that demand for music instruction tends to fluctuate based on interest level. Rhythm games like Guitar Hero and Rock Band sparked a lot of interest in people and their desire to learn an instrument. However, that didn't last. There are still new instrument-based games coming out, but the overall attraction just isn't what it used to be.

Bottom line: there will *always* be a need for music teachers, but there are external factors that could affect your income.

Attitude

To be successful in any endeavour, I believe it's important to have the right mindset and attitude. Music instruction is no exception.

I think the best advice I can give is to be as enthusiastic and on-fire for your instrument(s) as possible. Then, bring that enthusiasm to your lessons. Have high expectations for your students, and don't be afraid to challenge them along the way. You attract what you are, so if you're willy-nilly about your own mindset, your students are likely to follow your example.

Let's explore these key points in a little more detail.

- **Enthusiasm:** enthusiasm is contagious. Some of your students may need to be reminded that they are there to have fun and to embark upon a thrilling journey of musical exploration. If they feel like they're at school, they're going to treat music lessons like they treat homework. That won't help them to get the most out of music lessons. Help them to see that music is a blast, and help them to catch that vision. Conversely, some students may need to be reminded that they are paying for your time. If they are wasting time, it's a sure sign that you are charging too little.

- **High expectations:** inevitably, you will run into students that won't show a lot of interest in music. Some won't practice. At that point, you have a choice. You can coast and let the reins loose, you can set the standards high and continue to expect excellence, or you can confront. In my experience, some lessons are equivalent to babysitting; the money you earn is the time the parents didn't have to look after their kid. It seems like music *should* be for everyone, but my experience would confirm otherwise. You can also confront the student about their lack of interest. Be careful; the idea here isn't to discourage your student. Your goal is to help them to realize that their gifting and talents may lie elsewhere, even if they haven't discovered them yet. Their music studies could potentially benefit their other studies or talents too.

- **Challenge:** students need to feel like they are making progress to stay in lessons. If they don't feel like they are getting better, then they will quit, even with evidence to the contrary. Some students may have a bit of an unrealistic expectation around how fast they can learn. If so, keep throwing more challenges at them. If they can keep up, they will almost certainly stay in lessons. Even if they can't, they should begin to set more realistic expectations for themselves.

- **Example:** if you are convicted about where you're going and what you intend to do, people will follow you. If not, there is going to be a limit to how well you can serve your students. The reality is that most of them won't ever exceed your level of playing. A large number will always be a step or two behind you. However, if you work to become a great role model, more students will follow your example. If you have a great practice habit, they will adopt that work ethic for themselves too. If you want your students to become all that they can be, then show them the way.

10 Essential Characteristics of Successful Music Instructors

If you want to become a music instructor and pursue it as a career, there are certain characteristics that you will need to cultivate. Some are *intangible*, which means you either have them or you don't. Not to say that these qualities cannot be developed, but they certainly can't be faked.

Let's take a closer look at what it takes to become a successful music instructor.

1) **Passion:** passion is an essential characteristic of a music instructor. However, when it comes to music and teaching, you can't really force it. Most of the time, you're either passionate about these things or you're not. As well, a passion for music doesn't always translate into a passion for teaching. A good teacher will have both. Passion can also mean the difference between feeling drained and burned out and feeling enthusiastic and optimistic at the end of the work day.

2) **Patience:** teaching is a process. Helping your students understand theory and musical concepts requires you to be patient and enduring. Not only will different students progress at different rates, they will also have different learning styles. You will have to tailor your lessons to suit the needs of the student, and be patient with them, even when they haven't practiced what they were assigned. If your students are younger, it's a good idea to get their parents involved whenever possible.

3) **Goal-oriented:** in order to help your students proceed at a pace that feels natural and progressive to them, you will have to help them set realistic goals and usher them towards achievement. By extension, you will also have to be goal-oriented. You can't tell your students what to do unless you are also doing it. Work towards becoming the best example of what is possible for their sake.

4) **Love of people/students:** teaching requires you to be others-focused. Depending on which career route you

take, the age of your students may vary, which does present some challenges. If you end up having to cater to a bigger age group, you will likely have to approach lessons a little differently depending on the age of the student. Regardless, people skills can only help you in this industry, and they are worth developing. If you want to be a great teacher, you will have to be a people person.

5) **Love of music:** a love of music should not be confused for passion, which was addressed earlier. You can be passionate about a particular genre or style of music, without really having a love and appreciation for every type of music. You never know what your students may require of you, so you will have to remain open to learning things you don't know. If you want to be a teacher, you should be prepared to learn and absorb a variety of different styles of music.

6) **Organizational skills:** whether you are teaching classes, workshops or individual lessons, you will need to be organized. You will need to take notes on each of your students and take the time to understand how you can best serve them. Because you will likely have to create or re-tool curriculums for each of your students, you will have to get in the habit of keeping track of all of them.

7) **Preparedness:** a good teacher will spend considerable amount of time in study and preparation before each lesson. It is usually fairly apparent when a teacher is winging it, and students tend not to respond to that

very well. Though lessons are generally student-driven, that doesn't negate the necessity for you to come prepared with material that your students can work on "by default". You need to have a backup plan for when they have no idea where to go or what to do next.

8) **Adaptive personality:** not all of your students will progress at the same rate. Some will be slower, some will be faster. Some will be better visual learners, while others will be better auditory learners. You have to have a willingness to adapt to, and work with every kind of student. Music can only be taught to an extent; after a certain point, it is up to the student to decide how far they want to take it. In short, you will have to learn to be adaptive depending on the student and the situation. At times, you may end up having to break the flow of a lesson to take your student or students in a different direction. Whatever the case, you will need to stay alert and figure out how you can best guide your students in the direction they need to go.

9) **A solid work ethic:** teachers need to have a solid work ethic to keep on top of all of their students. Let's say, for example, that you needed to learn an entire guitar solo for one of your students for their next lesson. In order to be able to do that in a timely manner, you need to have the skills to be able to break the solo down into pieces and learn it quickly. You also need to be willing to work hard to get it done. It may seem like a lot of pressure in the short term, but in the long term it will

also benefit your playing, so it's a one-stone, two-bird situation.

10) **Logistical skills:** if you are pursuing the private instruction route, you will need to be able to organize your schedule and have a solid handle on logistics. This is especially true if you have to drive from one home to another. You will need to account for and create some margin for driving times, breaks and meals.

Conclusion

It has often been said that if you want to master something, you should teach it. I don't know if I totally agree with that sentiment, but teaching definitely does help to reinforce the concepts you already know and understand. Due to the fact that teaching always involves other people, you will likely have to work on your people skills as well.

One of the paradoxes of instruction is that the best players don't necessarily make for the best teachers. A teacher has to be able to simplify and break down concepts for their students. They have to keep a beginner's mindset, and remember what it was like to be new to the instrument. If you want to grow to become a great teacher, this is a requirement.

In an ideal world, a teacher will have both skill and passion. If you don't see it as a career, then you won't necessarily require both.

What I Like

- ➤ **Workshops:** some of my favourite teaching experiences have occurred at group lessons and/or workshops, because they energize me. I guess it could be because there is an element of *performance* to it. You have to connect with the people in front of you and you have to establish yourself as a credible source of information. Workshops also tend to pay a lump sum that you simply cannot earn in individual lessons.

- ➤ **Connections:** I really enjoyed building friendships with my students as well as other teachers. Some have even become long-term friends. Regardless of the situation, it's almost always the people you remember and treasure, and not the work or the event itself.

- ➤ **Opportunity:** you never know when new opportunities might come to you as result of teaching. They might come directly through your students, or if you teach at a store, they might even come from the manager or other employees, especially if that store is considered a community hub. You will likely learn about local music venues and events, and you might even have the chance to open for another band that is headed by one of your colleagues.

What I Don't Like

- ➤ **Exhaustion:** let's face it; nobody likes burning out. I think teaching tends to use a lot of mental and emotional energy. If you are able to pace yourself, or you just love working with people, it may energize you, but otherwise it's good to know that teaching will demand something of you, like any work.

> **In-home lessons:** there are some companies that offer in-home lessons to their clients. Teachers are required to drive to the homes of their students and teach them on-site. Typically, you can make more money this way, but you may end up driving a lot more too. If you live in a smaller town or a dense city, this probably won't prove to be as big of an issue. If you are in a bigger city, however, it can get out of hand fast. You also have to think about the fact that you will be spending more money on gas and car maintenance, almost negating any extra money you might earn.

Action Steps

> **Decide:** determine whether or not teaching is something you want to do; part-time or full-time. Keep in mind that you will often be working evenings and weekends, when you might prefer to record or write songs. If you love teaching, however, you will love these hours, because your days will be free. Or, if you do choose to teach in a school, you will have more time in the evenings and the weekends.

> **Commit:** if you've decided to become a teacher, commit to learning more about music and your instrument on a daily basis. Not only will this help you with your lessons, you will also become a better musician in the process. Should you choose to do

something other than teaching down the line; more knowledge can only help you.

➢ **Create a lesson book:** though you may have to approach every lesson a little differently, you will still find it useful to store all of your lessons, handouts and curriculums in one place. You could use a binder, a spiral notebook, a moleskine, or whatever works for you. A binder works great, because you can always add or remove pages later on. One of the reasons to have a lesson book is so that you can refer to it when you're not sure where to take one of your students next.

10. Copywriting

Let us prove to the world that good taste, good art, and good writing can be good selling. - William Bernbach

Hold on a second - I'm not in advertising.

That thought may enter your mind as you begin to explore this chapter.

True, a musician is not *exclusively* in advertising, nor is copywriting in their job description (if there is such a thing).

However, I still hold to the notion that every piece of writing you publish (online or off) is important. Your band bio is meant to elicit interest and excitement. Your social posting is supposed to engage and hold the attention of your followers. Your website should be converting visitors into subscribers or buyers.

Certainly, design elements, images and pictures are important too, but what's one of the first elements people connect with on your website (or in an ad, for that matter)? It's *the words you use*.

Words have power.

Copywriting is about recognizing this power and using it to get the kind of response you want from people.

It's about understanding people's motives and the psychology behind their actions. It's about being persuasive and convincing in your marketing.

I have no doubt that you've read copy that is anything but persuasive or convincing. In fact, I'm almost certain that there are examples within this book that people could point to. It's something I'm working on.

A passive voice can make your copy ineffective. A lack of confidence can make it fizzle.

Here's a very simple comparison between the active and passive voice:

Passive voice: the book was picked up by Melissa who read it in one day.

Active voice: Melissa picked up the book and read it in one day.

The difference is small, and there is a place for a passive voice, but when the voice is active, people tend to feel more engaged. In copy, there is little room for a passive voice.

This is the art of copywriting.

Introduction to Copywriting

So what exactly is copywriting?

Copywriting generally refers to **the writing of any sales or marketing script that is carefully crafted to compel the reader to action** (if you need an example, go to the Apple website and read the taglines next to any product; oh, and careful not to spend money you don't have while you're there).

Although I am using the term "copywriting" in a broader sense here, as in *any piece of text you write*, the aforementioned definition still applies a lot of the time. The purpose of your text, in general, is to get people to take action. Therefore, you have to become a better copywriter. Or, you have to find someone who can do it for you.

Spelling & Grammar

One of the core reasons any piece of text ceases to be as effective as it could be is due to poor spelling and grammar. I have heard Andrew Dubber say that people who don't take the time to spell-check their documents could prove to be unreliable in other ways. Wow. That means that the performance of any of your campaigns could also be affected by your "creative spelling".

Let's face it; no one is perfect. Even though I feel very comfortable with the English language, I still take the time and care to spell-check, read, and re-read any copy that I write. At the very least, I would advise running your text – especially text that will appear on your website – through a spellchecker.

You're a musician, not a copywriter. I get it. If you intend to do all the writing for you or your band, however, you're going to have to get good at it. If you intend to communicate and engage with your fans, send emails, ask for gigs, work with a promoter... *anything*. You'll want to get good at communication and writing effective copy.

Band or Artist Bio

I could probably write an entire page, if not an entire chapter on the subject of an effective bio. However, I'm going to keep this section on the succinct side. I have also talked about writing bios on my blog and podcast in more detail, so if this just isn't enough, you could always go there (http://www.dawcast.com/) for more.

I have often said that the best bio is a *copy and paste bio* and I still believe that to be the case. Any bio that you couldn't see running in a local newspaper, blog post, press release, or music magazine is not ready to go on your website. It just... *slows things down*.

If a media person is looking for your bio and doesn't find what they're looking for, or they discover that it's poorly written, they are likely to pass you up for someone else. They might not be back to your website, period. Opportunity missed.

Why? Because they probably don't have a lot of time to re-write, edit, research, or tweak your bio. If they're a journalist, they're not going to take the risk of looking bad by publishing a lacklustre bio as-is either. That's why your bio should be *copy and paste ready*. It should already contain all of the important details.

Take a moment to think from the reader's perspective. What information would *you* like to see in a bio? Here are some suggestions:

1) **Names of all band members and the instruments they play**: sure, you know all your band members by name and what role they play in the band, but media people don't necessarily have a lot of time to poke around to find out. Make this information obvious, even if it's not directly part of your written bio (i.e. headshots with names and instruments underneath). It's good practice to credit the photographers who took the photos as well.

2) **Geographical location**: another rather obvious thing media people want to know is where you're from. It's fine to talk about places you've performed at or where you originally hail from, but ultimately you need to stress where you're currently active.

3) **What you sound like/genre**: the reader of your bio usually wants to get a sense of what you sound like. Even if you have to make a separate column for your influences, genre(s) or what you sound like, make sure the information is readily available. I realize that a lot of musicians don't want to be pigeonholed, but providing this information takes a lot of the guesswork out of the equation. Suppose a music reviewer wanted to review your album. If you had a list of influences and genre qualifications, you would be helping the reviewer save a lot of time because they wouldn't have to go searching their brain, music library and Google for what and who you sound like. Likewise, an event planner is going to have an easier time figuring out if your music is suited

to their occasion or venue. I don't see any downside to cooperating with the people who can move your career forward.

4) **A compelling story**: a bio is not merely the dumping place for a long list of credentials and accomplishments. It might help to include a couple of quotes from industry greats (if you have any) or list a couple of festivals you've played at, but if a bio is reduced to a list, it's not a bio. *A bio should tell a story*. If your band is made up of relatives or family members, make the reader aware of that upfront. If one of your band members lived in a foreign country, write about that. Find something that is going to stick out in people's minds and emphasize it.

5) **Contact information**: if you're following my train of thought, I shouldn't even have to tell you why including your contact information is so important. Suppose an album reviewer wanted to ask you a question. Suppose a venue owner wanted to book your band. Having this information readily available *at the end of your bio* would make it easy for interested parties to contact you. They wouldn't have to go digging through the rest of your site either.

Press Releases

A press release is simply a 300 - 500 word article that outlines a newsworthy story. Press releases are sometimes turned into bigger news items by the media, if the story is compelling enough.

I have personally used press releases to help promote a couple of my shows in the past.

There was one time I booked a show at a humble coffee house. The manager agreed to have me in to play, but she said she couldn't guarantee an audience. However, they would collect emails on my behalf and alert those people when I was coming to play. What a wonderful gesture.

To reciprocate, I decided to publish a press release detailing how the show had come about, and how it would help to stimulate local business. This got me a listing in the city events and the coffee shop was bulging with traffic all day long. The manager gave me a card and thanked me later with tears welling up. I don't think I sold any CDs or had many newsletter signups that day, but that was thanks enough.

Another show that I promoted using a press release was a show I did for a grand opening of another coffee shop. Although I didn't have much of an angle to work with on that one, the grand opening was still well-attended, and I got to perform for quite a few people. It was also a paid gig.

If my press releases had been poorly written, would I have enjoyed the same results I experienced? Had I not worked the business angle, would anyone have cared? It's possible, but they probably would not have cared to the same degree that they did. I have learned that press releases are a very powerful tool for announcing important shows, tours, and album releases. I don't recommend spamming releases with every news item you have, but for particularly important events, it is definitely worthwhile.

Here are some specific tips you can follow to create effective press releases:

- **Make sure it's newsworthy:** does your press release tell a story? Are you using it to share something that the media is going to be interested in? If not, then you either need to find a new angle, rewrite your article, or scrap it altogether. Some press release distributors won't even publish your article unless they deem that it is, in fact, *news*. Make sure to pick your moments. An album release, a tour announcement, an award ceremony... these would all be examples of release-worthy events.

- **Observe the guidelines:** different distributors have different policies and guidelines you need to follow. Ultimately, you can do whatever you want with your press release (i.e. email it to people you know), but if you want to publish it through a distributor (recommended), you're going to need to make sure to abide by their terms of use. Remember to look into this before submitting your article. A distributor can help you to get your news item out to a variety of different outlets, and may be able to get you more exposure than you would be able to on your own. If you're going to take advantage of the tools available to you, then be conscious of their guidelines.

- **Stick to the format:** there is a specific format that press releases generally follow. The good news is that some distributors already have your bases covered. All you have to do is enter your headline and article body, and they will take care of the rest. But, just in case you encounter a site that requires you to follow the conventional format, there's an article via Music Biz Academy that explains how to write a press release (to access this resource, go to: **http://dawcast.com/the-new-music-industry-resource-list/**). Regardless of the exact specifics, as I mentioned earlier, your article should be within the 300 - 500 word range. Make sure to get to the point, and avoid filler. Copywriting is just as much about the absence of text as it is the presence of text. Some words can be cut out completely.

- **Check your spelling and grammar:** again, this is pretty basic stuff, but it's still important. Make sure your article is free of any blatant errors. Sometimes, regardless of errors, your release will be sent out to multiple outlets. By that time, it's too late to make any corrections. Be sure to take care of it upfront.

- **Use your press releases to educate and inform:** the paradoxical nature of a press release is such that while it is used as a promotional tool to make the world aware of recent happenings, it isn't merely for marketing. The primary purpose of a press release is to educate and inform the reader. You shouldn't be using it as a means to pitch. Any promotion you receive is just a healthy side benefit of making your reader aware of a newsworthy event. The press is always looking for interesting stories, so that's just one way a press release can be value-adding.

- **Know who you are writing for:** press releases can be sent out in a variety of different ways. Whether you're looking to send it to a specific publication, email it to your media connections or use a distributor to get it out there, you should have your end reader in mind as you put your pen to paper (or fingers to keyboard as the case may be). If you're going to submit your release to a distributor, you aren't so much concerned with what the distributor is going to think about it as you are trying to appeal to a specific kind of reader. For example, if you know that a certain magazine consistently reads press releases that pop up on a particular blog, then you need to write your article in a matter that's going to get their attention.

- **Include quotes:** quotes are particularly useful in making a release come alive. Of course, it can be kind of tricky for an artist or a band to come up with a citation without quoting themselves. At times, this can still work, but at other times it can look pretty tacky. If you have someone that's writing press releases for you, then it's definitely less of an issue. You can have them interview you and pick out the most juicy, most engaging quotes. If the news item involves others in some way, that should also open up some opportunities to get some quotes.

>> Tools & Tips

To access these and other resources, go to:
http://dawcast.com/the-new-music-industry-resource-list/

> ➢ **PRWeb:** if you don't want to mess around and you just want to get the job done, I recommend using PRWeb for distributing your press releases. Unless they have a special going on, you can expect to pay at least $99 (more if you choose to have your release publicized to additional outlets) to have your release distributed, but the service is well worth the price as they target many major news outlets.

> ➢ For every great service or tool, there is typically a cheaper, less effective option. If you want to send out press releases for free, there are some sites that allow you to do so. I once used 24-7 Press Release, and it was relatively effective, but it doesn't look like they allow you to use their service for free anymore. However, it isn't particularly hard to find free services with a quick Google search. In particular, I recommend Press Exposure.

13 Ways to Become a Better Copywriter

So your goal may not be to become a master copywriter; that's completely understandable.

On the other hand, maybe this is something you get excited about. Maybe you could see yourself pursuing copywriting a little further.

Since we are discussing music entrepreneurship, you may even be able to find an interesting niche by combining your interest in music and copywriting.

Regardless, I don't think it would hurt any musician to know a little bit about writing copy. Writing is a valuable skill, and as I've already demonstrated, an *absolute must* for every career-minded musician.

Here are 13 ways to become a better copywriter:

1) **Read:** if you want to become a better copywriter, you should be delving into a lot of articles and books. And no, you can't cheat by listening to audiobooks (though you might want to listen to those too). You *have* to get in the habit of reading, even if it isn't something you particularly enjoy. As far as what to read, just about any material can help you to grow, but because there are so many resources out there that talk specifically about copywriting, that should be your main focus. Really take the time to study the material you learn and figure out how you can apply it to your own copywriting efforts.

2) **Practice what you learn:** while it is good to absorb information, if you don't put it to use, it's just knowledge. Knowledge is power, but only when you act upon it. If you're going to spend a significant amount of time in study anyway, you might as well find a way to use what you learn. Everything takes practice, and unless you practice, you're not going to get better automatically. So take the techniques you learn and try them out. They may not all work the first time around, but that's exactly why you need practice. Don't give up if you encounter some failure.

3) **Determine who your audience is:** a copywriter always has to keep their audience in mind. Effective copy is built on a solid understanding of who the reader is. Naturally, this is going to take some practice. For example, if you're interested in getting exposure for your news items, you'll have to get a sense of who covers music related news and what they're interested in. If you want to convert more fans with an ad, you should have a pretty good idea of who your existing fans are. It all depends on who you're talking to. This is a good thing to keep in mind regardless of whether we're talking about copywriting or not.

4) **Write from the perspective of the prospect:** in other words, you need to write for your audience and not just for yourself. The purpose of copywriting is generally to sell a product or a service, so a copywriter has to know why their prospect is going to be interested in what they are selling. Again, for the intents and purposes of this

book, I'm referring to copywriting as *any text you write for the sake of your music career,* but that doesn't really change this principle. You still need to think about your value proposition. You still need to see things from the perspective of your fan or the journalist or event planner.

5) **Reflect:** we may very well be one of the least reflective generations there is. That might be because we've forgotten how valuable reflection is. Reflection allows you to interpret the events in your life, find meaningful answers, and figure out how you can change for the better or do things differently in the future. A master copywriter will make it a point to practice every single day, and then reflect on what they have learned. You may not have the inclination or time to become a master in the field, and that's okay. The point here is to get better at reflecting on what you have learned. Deliberately set aside some time in your calendar if you have to. This is a valuable activity regardless of what undertaking you're involved in.

6) **Seek coaching and training:** I've already stressed the importance of mentorship in this book, and I'm sure it's starting to hit home. If you want to become a better copywriter, you should learn from the best. It's great to learn and study on your own, but when you have coaching from a pro, your skill will be brought to a whole new level. When you have someone training you, you also have the opportunity to have a conversation. Feedback is extremely valuable, and if your coach is

invested in your future, they will definitely take the time to point out what you're doing right and what areas you can improve in.

7) **Get your mindset right:** you can have all the skill in the world, but without the right mindset, it's hard to write good copy. It's really the same regardless of what you're trying to write, whether it's a blog post, a bio, or an ad. At times, you may feel creatively drained. You might lack inspiration. You might be under pressure to get a project done. Always remember that your mind is under your control. You can make up your mind up to do whatever you want, and even if you're not *feeling* inspired, you can still sit yourself down in front of a word processor to write. It doesn't matter if it's good or not; that's what editing is for. Furthermore, you can always scrap whatever you don't like. A good copywriter probably does just as much purging as they do writing. Be prepared to overcome mental blocks and creative drought.

8) **Dare to go deeper:** a master copywriter is likely well-versed in fields other than just copywriting. Psychology, marketing, storytelling, sales and other similar topics tend to compliment copywriting. You may not have any aspirations towards becoming a master copywriter, but these are also really valuable things to know and understand as a musician. If you don't, you most certainly need someone in your corner that does. Psychology, marketing, storytelling, sales... sound

familiar? That's because that's what a huge chunk of this book is about!

9) **Be goal-oriented:** before you write any copy, make sure to get clear on *why* you are writing it. Copy is used to get your audience to take action, so think about what you want your reader to do. Copy is much more effective when you have an end goal in mind. If you begin randomly and end randomly, all of your precious text is for nothing. When you know what you're trying to achieve, you will find it much easier to build towards that objective.

10) **Write compelling headlines:** the beginning of your article is often the most important part. That's why headlines, subject lines, or titles are so vital. You need to catch the attention of the reader, and make them want to read the rest of your piece. Again, this is usually a matter of seeing things from the perspective of the reader. What benefit will they gain by reading your piece? Why should they be interested in it? Answer these questions upfront, and you will keep readers engaged.

11) **Include quotes where applicable:** we've already talked about the benefit of quotes in your copy, but it's worth mentioning again. If you're writing an ad, then there's nothing quite as powerful as a customer testimony. It lends a significant amount of credibility to your copy. If you're looking to get booked in more venues, a quote from an event planner might be useful. If you are putting together a press release for your new album, a

quote from a fan or a reviewer could be a huge value-add. A well-placed quote can enhance your copy.

12) **Don't be afraid to edit:** again, good copy gets to the point. You don't want stuffing or filler. Your copy should be tight, clean and succinct. Become a merciless editor. Edit, edit and edit until all of the extraneous text is gone. We tend to use a lot of filler words in speech, and there might be a good reason to do that, but when you're trying to communicate a message through copy, the fewer words you can use to express it eloquently the better.

13) **Find professional copy you like and write it out by hand:** this is a proven way to become a better copywriter. If you've read an ad that caught your attention, or a sales letter that stays with you long after you've read it, you may want to copy it out word-for-word by hand. This helps you to get in the mindset of the writer who created that copy. It helps you to understand what their goal was, and what made their copy so impactful. It may sound time-consuming and tedious, and to a degree it certainly is, but it's a really great way to improve your skills as a copywriter.

Conclusion

Several other areas where copywriting might apply are blogging, social media and video. Fortunately, I have entire chapters dedicated to those topics, so you are sure to find more relevant information there.

Hopefully, you're starting to figure out how much writing work is involved in building a music career. Previous to this, you may have been under the impression that there isn't a lot of forethought put into something as simple as a bio, but the reality is that the written word is one of the most vital forms of communication. Effective music marketing relies upon words that match a brand, and that takes thought.

If you feel overwhelmed, keep in mind that you don't have to do this all yourself. Yes, you may have to handle it all in the beginning, but as you meet more people and your network grows, you should be able to find people that can help you or give you valuable feedback along the way.

Allow me to illustrate this point by sharing a story with you. Believe it or not, The Music Entrepreneur website would not be what it is today if not for Tim Francis (sounds a bit like Tim Ferriss, but it's a different guy; however, Tim is also a successful businessperson).

I had a chance to chat with Tim because of my work. I do pre-interviews and create show outlines for a podcast that shall go unnamed, and one of the people that I got to talk to was Tim.

If not for my work, I'm not sure that I would have ever had a chance to chat with Tim, and that would have been a shame, because he actually lives in Edmonton, Alberta, a mere three hours away (by car) from where I live!

Anyway, we happened to have a little bit of extra time left over when we finished the pre-interview, so when I told Tim about my website, he was happy to give me some advice. He is primarily a marketing guy, so he has a good handle on the elements that make a website look credible and trustworthy.

I wish I could have chatted with him for longer, but either way the tips he gave me were gold. I used them to make some much needed changes to The Music Entrepreneur, and that's how it got to be where it's at today.

I added credibility badges, I changed the name of the site, I picked a new color scheme, and I made my call to actions obvious. The website essentially went through an entire redesign.

Bottom line, you just never know when or how you might cross paths with people that can propel you forward. Success occurs where opportunity and preparedness meet, so if you want to be successful, make sure to **be prepared**!

What I Like

I'm an avid reader and writer, so it's probably no surprise that I also like copywriting.

Any time I'm reading an article or a book, I'm on the alert for errors. That may not always be a good thing, as it can put me in a space where I'm critical of what I'm reading. However, that's also what makes me a good editor.

I have edited copy for websites, email campaigns, blog posts, books, and other items for various individuals and businesses.

To some extent, I probably need to get over myself, because bad writing tends to turn me off, even if what's being said in the piece is actually value-adding. If the information is useful, it doesn't have to be perfect, right?

Ultimately, that's my message to you too. Your writing doesn't have to be perfect. Perfection is probably going to get in the way of you accomplishing what you want to.

What I Don't Like

There isn't anything in particular I don't like about copywriting, though I will say that it takes significant thought, time and effort.

Going back a few years, writing a blog post meant putting together a 500 to 600 word article, and that was enough for you to get indexed and ranked in search.

These days, the competition is so fierce that long form content is getting featured more often. 2,000 to 3,000 word blog posts are not uncommon.

More writing means more thought, and a good chunk of online marketing these days relies upon writing.

So, whether I'm writing a book, a blog post, a bio or a press release, putting my thoughts into written form isn't always the easiest thing to do. At the end of the day, I still enjoy it though.

Action Steps

> **Understand the basics of copywriting:** if you walk away with nothing else from this chapter, make sure you understand the basics of copywriting. When you

know what purpose it serves, you are well on your way to developing great content assets for your band.

➢ **Consider how your brand connects with the words you use:** whether or not you are aware of it, you have a brand. That brand has the chance to be enhanced by the words you use. Color schemes, clothing and instrument choices, words... all of these things factor into your overall brand. To create a cohesive and effective package, look at it from all angles, including the words you use to describe your music.

➢ **Ask for feedback:** if you have no idea how your words are connecting (or aren't connecting) with your fans, ask them! Get their opinion on your ads, your bio, your blog posts, your website, your press releases, and so forth. Your fans are already relating to you because of who and what you are, and they are almost certainly connecting with your words in one way or another.

➢ **Look for help:** realistically, you can't do it all alone. Seek out those who are good at writing, and ask for their help. Involve them in your projects, and seek to understand their approach.

11. Blogging

> **"** If you love writing or making music or blogging or any sort of performing art, then do it. Do it with everything you've got. Just don't plan on using it as a shortcut to making a living. - Seth Godin

For all intents and purposes, I've been blogging before it was even *called* blogging. I set up my first website in 97/98 and I've been developing and writing for the web ever since. That means that I've been creating online content since I was 14.

I started writing when I could barely even put cohesive sentences together. To put that sentence in proper context, you should know that I grew up in Japan. When I returned to Canada, I still had to learn to read and write properly. I'm glad I did it though, because I definitely improved over time. I kept studying the language, increasing my vocabulary, continually aspiring to be like the authors and writers I admired.

If you're not a great writer yourself, I believe you're either going to need to develop those skills or find someone who can help you (you can hire me, but I don't come cheap). Here's the thing: there's quite a bit of writing involved in building a music career; *more than you'd think*. I'm sure you're starting to get the picture if you read the previous chapter on copywriting, but it's worth reiterating.

You need to write a bio. You need to write blog posts. You need to create additional content for your website. You need to write press releases. And that's just scratching the surface.

You have to do a good job of it too. A poorly written bio won't do you any favours. If nothing else, your bio has to be good.

I'm fortunate in that I've been on both sides of the booking equation; I've been the artist looking for the gig, and I've been the event planner booking the artist. There's a lot of clarity that comes from experiencing both sides, and if you have the chance to do so, I would definitely recommend it. Let's just say that I've seen my fair share of poorly written bios while looking for acts to book. In some cases, I've still booked those artists, but I could tell their bio really wasn't doing them any favours.

In any case, let's delve into the different components of writing as a musician.

>> Tools & Tips

To access these and other resources, go to:
http://dawcast.com/the-new-music-industry-resource-list/

> **Booking Shows:** if you'd like to learn more about planning events, I discuss the advantages of booking for yourself and booking for others in this podcast audio.

Introduction to Blogging

It has to be acknowledged that blogging in itself is a very, very saturated medium. However, the purpose of blogging as a musician is to keep the content on your site fresh and engage with your audience, not necessarily to become a professional blogger or enhance your site's SEO value (unless that's part of your online strategy). Blogging is the easiest way to keep your site updated. You don't have to mess around with HTML and CSS code to update a blog (although if you want to customize your site's design, acquiring some basic coding skills couldn't hurt), and you don't have to manually archive your site's content either.

The great thing about being an artist is that creating an audience for your blog - at least in some ways - should prove easier than starting out as a blogger without a niche or a plan. True fans of yours can't wait to learn more about you or hear your new single or watch your new video. Blogging is a supplemental activity for an artist; it should be a smaller part of a bigger strategy. Be forewarned though; if you've never blogged before, it can be pretty addicting.

> ## >> Tools & Tips
>
> To access these and other resources, go to:
> **http://dawcast.com/the-new-music-industry-resource-list/**
>
> ➤ **SEO:** in case you don't know what SEO is, the

acronym stands for **Search Engine Optimization**. It's the practice of configuring the pages and posts on your website so that they will be displayed more prominently in search results on search engines like Google. The idea is to choose your target keywords and build your content around them. SEO used to refer to tactics for gaming the system, but those types of tricks don't really work anymore, and could get you penalized in search.

➢ **WordPress:** whether you're an experienced blogger or a complete beginner, one of the best platforms to get started on is WordPress. Not only is it free, some web hosts allow you to install it with a single click! You should be aware that there are two different versions; you can go to WordPress.org and download a copy to install on your site, or you can go to WordPress.com and set up a free blog. For all intents and purposes, I recommended installing the platform on your website, because it is more customizable and professional.

Create a Blogging Schedule

Figure out upfront whether you're going to blog daily, three times a week, once per week, bi-weekly or monthly. I wouldn't recommend posting any less than that, as the effectiveness of blogging less than once a month is pretty suspect. Once you've figured out how often you're going to post, commit to publishing new content on an ongoing basis. There are ways of making this happen even if you have a busy touring or recording schedule (more on that later). Consistency is of the essence here. You'll want to commit to regular posting before you even get started.

I've personally stopped and started so many times it's not even funny. Don't use me as the model example of a consistent blogger. I'm merely telling you what I think should be the standard to shoot for.

>> Tools & Tips

To access these and other resources, go to: **http://dawcast.com/the-new-music-industry-resource-list/**

➢ **Google Calendar:** if you're worried that your intention to keep a blogging schedule might slip through the cracks, consider using Google Calendar to have notifications sent to your phone. That way, you can always remind yourself before you run out of fresh content.

➢ **Google Drive:** with Google Drive, you can create folders, documents, presentations, spreadsheets, forms and drawings. Documents that you create in Google Drive can then be shared with your team members too.

Have a Content (Marketing) Strategy

I knew that I should be blogging as a musician, and I was, but oftentimes I just couldn't figure out exactly *what* to post. The irony of the matter is that I usually had numerous other blogs (and by that I mean *separate* sites) at any given time (not recommended if you're serious about building a music career, although it can be beneficial to create a *sister site* of sorts) and posted a lot of content on those sites. I should have figured out earlier that I could have just as easily posted those same things on my music site, even if they were not directly related to music.

So the lesson here is: **come up with a content strategy** so you can keep your blogging efforts focused. You're going to want to post about your music and your band, so do that, but also be prepared with other fun and engaging things. Post random photos, retrospectives, tour diaries, concert write-ups, album reviews (of other bands), interview transcripts, funny or interesting videos or anything else you personally have interest in.

Your fans already love your music, but I'm sure they would also like to know more about *you*. Get comfortable posting about things you like, your activities, your personal life, your sense of style, etc. Keep a list of ideas on hand at all times, because, trying to come up with new ideas on a regular basis can be difficult. I have a folder on my desktop labelled 'Post Ideas' in which I store all of my notes and, of course, post ideas.

You may find it helpful to come up with *blogging themes* as well. For example, you could post photos one week, post a video the next and post a tour diary the week after that. People tend to like *organized* content. When you consistently post about the same things on a regular basis, it builds up anticipation with your audience and trust for your brand.

Of course, blogging also has SEO (Search Engine Optimization) benefits. What this means is that text-based content is keyword rich, containing many words, phrases and tags that pertain to your subject matter. That's all well and good, but again you're not necessarily competing with other music bloggers. Plus, you won't necessarily make more fans by ranking high in Google. It's still nice to know that if you put a little time into it, you can be the first relevant result on Google for your band name. Be sure to register your *dot com domain name* and aspire to make it the first search result in Google above any of your social media sites.

For those who do want to make blogging a bigger part of their strategy, knowing the previous points certainly couldn't hurt. It is possible to maximize your exposure utilizing your blog, and I don't want to downplay that aspect of it at all. I think some semblance of balance is important if you intend to write and record and market great songs too, though.

>> Tools & Tips

To access these and other resources, go to:
http://dawcast.com/the-new-music-industry-resource-list/

➢ **Sister site:** I mentioned the *sister site* concept at the beginning of this section, and I believe I originally got it from David Nevue's book, *How to Promote Your Music Successfully on the Internet*, which is definitely a recommended read. Nevue is a six-figure musician who writes and records solo piano and also offers sheet music for sale on his website. The sister site concept is definitely for advanced users, and probably won't be for everyone. In essence, you can create a *related* website, one that offers music lessons, music industry news, career advice, or other relevant content that closely intersects with what you do. Having another website gives you the ability to cross-promote and draw in a new audience. Both of your sites can benefit from the ping-pong traffic, and done right, you can build up added credibility. The tricky part is in maintaining and updating two sites at the same time. If possible, collaborate on this project with others and endeavour to make the website a valuable resource for others. Otherwise, it might actually hurt your efforts.

> **How to Develop a Workflow for Your Blogging Efforts**: this post examines Darren Rowse's approach to creating a blogging workflow. It's important to develop efficient methods that work for you, and this post may help you to identify some strategies.

Content Marketing Trifecta

At this point, I want to touch briefly on what I call the content marketing trifecta. One of the ways companies are driving traffic to their websites is by producing stimulating, engaging content and getting it out to different social channels or popular websites and apps. They are bringing visitors in by providing interesting articles, guides, podcast episodes and videos.

In layman's terms, it looks like this:

If you want to **generate** traffic from Google, and increase your site's ranking and appeal to the readers out there, write blog posts and relevant articles.

If you want to build a traffic source from iTunes and appeal to auditory learners, then produce podcast episodes. Podcast episodes can later be transcribed and published as blog posts as well.

If you want to take advantage of the second most used search engine on the planet and appeal to visual learners, create videos for YouTube. You can re-purpose the audio for a podcast episode, or transcribe the discourse and publish it as a blog post as well.

As you can see, leveraging these three content types can extend your reach to different audiences, and they complement each other very well besides. Podcasting and video marketing are covered in more detail in later chapters.

>> Tools & Tips

To access these and other resources, go to: **http://dawcast.com/the-new-music-industry-resource-list/**

> ➤ **Content Marketing Trifecta:** The *Content Trifecta* concept comes from creative entrepreneur Pat Flynn, and is one of the strategies he employs in what he refers to as *being everywhere*. Quite simply, if your content can be found on popular platforms across the internet, you can reach a larger number of people who consume content in a variety of different ways. Flynn has a video that covers this subject in more detail. Access the link from the resource page and skip to 1:03:43 to hear him

discuss the Content Trifecta concept.

> In this section I mentioned that you can have your podcast episodes or videos **transcribed**. There are various sites like Elance and Upwork out there where you can outsource or hire virtual assistants to do this for you. I recommend using SpeechPad as I have found it to be quite reliable. The cost of transcription is generally $1.00 per minute of audio. As it pertains to transcription, it's nice to have a flat, predictable per-minute cost.

> **OneLoad:** using OneLoad, you can distribute your videos to a variety of video sharing websites more efficiently. I will be talking more about this later.

Schedule Posts

If you're using WordPress, it's easy to schedule posts for future dates. There are a couple of other blogging platforms that allow you to do this, but with the way things are going right now, there isn't much point in using anything but WordPress. If you've decided that you want to post weekly, you could easily set up a month's worth (or more) of posts well in advance of them ever being published. If you know you're going to be crunched for time over the next few weeks or even months, take a little extra time to work up a *blog post buffer*. Once your posts are scheduled, your site gets updated without you even being there to do it, which is a beautiful thing.

Why Blog?

Maybe you're not convinced. Maybe you don't see the point in blogging. It's really akin to saying, "Why should I have a Facebook *page*? I already have a profile." And if you don't know why that's a problem, here's the difference: with a Facebook page, you can rack up 'likes'. You can only tally up 'friends' with a profile. With a Facebook page, you can develop your brand, post your bio, link back to your website. You can do some of those things with your profile too, but it's bound to get lost in the clutter. Moreover, your profile is designed to host your *personal information*. How likely are you to add a stranger as a friend? What if that "stranger" is a record executive, only you don't know that yet? The *public* can access a Facebook page (depending on the settings). They can see *all* of the content. They can 'like' your band. They can contact your band directly. You can still leverage your personal profile for marketing purposes, but I wouldn't make it the destination for all things pertaining to your band.

When you actively blog about your activities, you don't have to rely on what others say about your music. A blog allows you to have more control over how you are perceived by the world. Blogging is a step up from social media. It's content that you actually own and have complete control over. In other words, if you're putting social media over blogging, you're missing the boat. All of your carefully crafted social media posts have a much shorter lifespan than your blog posts, which could hold their value three, four, five years (or longer) down the line depending on the content.

Sure, writing a blog post may seem like a bigger time-sink, but people engage with blogs differently than they do with social media. Moreover, the two connect well with each other. Everything you post to your blog can be shared on your social profiles. I would advise engaging those who want to consume their content in text form. You may find a new group of fans this way if you haven't started already.

Comments

Occasionally, you will probably have fans that interact with you on your blog and leave comments. Be prepared to engage with them and facilitate the discussion. At the very, *very* least, respond to the first comment in every thread.

Also note: you may not always get comments. You may not have a lot of comments. That doesn't mean your time is spent in vain. It doesn't mean your posts aren't getting read. Keep posting for the sake of the people who return to your website and *keep them coming back*.

You can have WordPress notify you by email when new comments are posted to your blog. Sadly, there are a lot of spammers out there, so unless you have sufficient security on your site, you may end up wasting time moderating comments from bots or hackers.

9 Things to Blog About As a Musician

Looking for a little inspiration?

There are a variety of different things you can blog about as a musician. In fact, when it comes down to it, you can blog about anything you want (more or less).

Therefore, my intention here isn't to fit your blogging efforts into a box. If anything, I hope to expand your thinking so you can see the possibilities unfold before you.

Blogging can achieve a lot of different things for you. It can extend your reach, help you to connect with more people, establish you as an authority as a subject, boost your search ranking, and so on.

With that in mind, ranking in Google shouldn't be your only goal. The time and effort spent on search engine optimization can be fruitless unless you're an algorithm junkie and you know exactly how to hack the system.

Engagement shouldn't be your only goal. If all you do is get lots of shares and comments on your posts, you might not be able to get people to take the next step with you. They'll keep coming back for your posts instead of subscribing to your newsletter or buying your merch or music.

Sharing news updates shouldn't be your only goal. That type of blogging tends to be boring, and people won't necessarily read what you have to say. Don't shy away from sharing exciting news, but don't get too caught up in your own world. You have to see things from the perspective of the reader.

Making money shouldn't be your only goal. Yes, blogging can lead people to connect with you and learn more about you, but if you focus too much on generating revenue from your website and your blog, you could end up alienating people and losing readers and/or fans!

I would love to say that there's a happy balance in there somewhere, but there really isn't. You have to experiment, try different things, and see what works for you.

None of the above goals are bad ones. In fact, they are all great things to aspire to. However, you should be aware of the downsides of blogging in addition to the upsides. That way, you can make better, more informed decisions.

If you need some ideas to get started, here are nine things you can start blogging about right away:

1) **Music you enjoy:** as you are surely aware, the music you listen to tends to influence your creative efforts; especially if you listen to it often. When you write about music you enjoy, you get to relate to people that also enjoy that music. By extension, they might take interest in your music as well. This could take a number of different forms. You could simply write about songs or artists you like. You could write music reviews. You could deconstruct songs and share your findings. You could blog about bands and artists your fans have said you sound like. You could put together lists of songs you like in a certain genre, or artists you'd like to one day collaborate with. You have a lot of options here.

2) **Your hobbies:** this may come as a surprise, but you are allowed to talk about things you enjoy other than music on your blog. Though music may be your main focus - and I know it's something you absolutely love doing - your fans would also like to hear about other things you enjoy. You could talk about movies, video games, food you like, or anything else that interests you. When I was invited by Corey Koehler to be on his podcast, he talked about the Vegan Black Metal Chef (who has quite the presence on YouTube). That's a really unique angle, and you might be able to find your own niche by smashing together your interests in a similar manner.

3) **Your live shows/tours:** you and I know that music isn't terribly glamorous most of the time, but that doesn't

mean your fans don't see it that way. Touring and live shows almost invariably provide you with interesting stories to share. Though it can be a little tiresome to add writing to your duties on tour, the amount of engagement you can get from these types of posts is incredible. I would encourage you to share photos, tell stories, and give your fans a behind-the-scenes look into your performance schedule.

4) **Your albums:** again, if you can show how the sausage is made, your fans will greatly appreciate it. This is why some bands have entire DVDs dedicated to individual recording projects. Even as a musician, I tend to enjoy these. Anyway, there are definitely ways to pull back the curtain through your blogging efforts too. You can talk about the process you go through to write your songs, what gear you used to record your latest album, what your thematic focus was, and so on.

5) **Your merch:** what's the best way to get people excited about your merch? To talk about it. Share why you're excited about the product, how it came to be, and what went into the design. Give an honest review of the quality and appeal of the merch item. If you want to do one better than that, take multiple photos of the product and share them alongside your post. If you want to go even deeper than that, get behind a video camera and film a video review. Keep in mind that an honest, detailed review is always best.

6) **Your gear:** again, what may seem ordinary to you is interesting and even exciting to your fans. Moreover,

there could be gear-heads coming to check out your website, in which case they're going to want to know what equipment you work with. You can also use the opportunity to share stories about your gear. The history of an instrument is often far more interesting than its specifications, though that can also be of interest to some.

7) **Local anything:** though your focus does not need to be entirely local, blogging about anything in your locality can get you noticed in a good way. After all, you have the opportunity to connect with anyone that lives in the same vicinity as you. You can talk to people directly and even work out cross-promotion deals if you want to. Restaurants, businesses, events and even fascinating people can all be subjects for your blog. Of course, you should exercise some discretion here. Please avoid talking about anyone or anything in a negative way, and don't feature people or businesses on your blog that don't want to be featured.

8) **Issues you care about:** musicians can be pretty outspoken and opinionated, so we have to be somewhat careful in how we broach this topic, but more than likely you have political, environmental, religious or other societal issues that your heart beats over. A musician has an opportunity to become a spokesperson for a cause, and this can be a good way of establishing identity. Of course, there can be some drawbacks too, so use some discretion in your approach.

9) **Interesting things you find across the internet:** as a blogger, you have the opportunity to turn your readers onto a variety of different things. We all tend to come across funny videos, cat GIFs, stunning photography, and the like. Your blog can be a good place to share the fascinating treasures you find on the web. Of course, you may have to ask for permission depending on what you are trying to share. Videos are generally free game (YouTube provides you with embed codes), but images can be a little finicky, so beware.

>> Tools & Tips

To access these and other resources, go to:
http://dawcast.com/the-new-music-industry-resource-list/

> ➤ **The Ultimate Guide to Blogging as a Musician:** fairly extensive but far from done, this post starts you at the basics, and takes you through the particulars of blogging as well as strategy and other great resources you can learn from.

Conclusion

There is so much more that could be said about blogging. I am barely even scratching the surface at this point. From WordPress plugins to marketing, it's a subject with a lot of depth. I hope that you will use this information as a jumping off point, and if you want to go deeper into this world, I would encourage you to continue to read up on the subject. Sites like ProBlogger and Copyblogger should serve you well.

What I Like

- ➢ **Movable Type:** Movable Type is another blogging platform much like WordPress. If you have competency in coding (HTML, CSS and a little bit of PHP) and you consider yourself an advanced user or webmaster, you might enjoy giving MT a try. There is definitely more documentation, tutorials and pre-designed themes available for WordPress, so unless you feel confident about your web development skills, you may not want to delve too far into it. If there's one thing I like about it, it's that customizing the look and feel of your website with MT is easier than tampering with WordPress themes (in my opinion). Unfortunately, as of the latest version, you have to pay for MT, and the price ranges aren't conducive to beginners. You can still download the older versions, but they probably won't be supported.

- ➢ **InfoBarrel:** since becoming an online marketer and content producer, I have found value in guest posting and writing articles for other websites. This allows me to create back-links to my site, which is one of many elements Google checks to determine your site's ranking. InfoBarrel is a **revenue sharing website** where you can write articles, earn a bit of money, and - as already noted - create back-links to your site in the process. There are other sites of a similar nature, but InfoBarrel is the only site I'm aware of that rewards you with 75% of the profits. You may or may not find any value in this tip unless you love writing, but I thought I would share it with you anyway, because it's something I like.

What I Don't Like

There really isn't a whole lot I don't like about blogging. I suppose lack of comments and feedback on a blog can be a little disheartening at times, but I've stopped looking at those metrics to decide whether I'm producing worthwhile content or not. It will probably factor into what I'm doing over the long haul, but I don't worry too much about it in the short-term.

Action Steps

Are you ready to take some action on the things you've learned in this chapter? You are free to use this list as a reference guide and come back to it later if you so choose. However, it is important to get in the habit of taking action, even when it seems a little scary at first.

> ➤ **Purchase a hosting plan:** the hosting plan I use is only $24.99 a month, so though it might seem expensive if you were to pay for several years upfront (i.e. $1499.40 for five years – not including taxes and other fees), it's really not that much when you consider everything you're getting (and you may not even understand everything you're getting). You can start with a plan that's as low as $5.99 per month, and for most people

that are just getting started, it should be more than sufficient. I suggest starting an account with Bluehost as I have really come to love their service.

➢ **Purchase and register a domain:** if you don't already have a domain name for your band, it's time to purchase one. This can typically be done through your web host, so if you choose to go with Bluehost, that is likely where you would go to purchase a domain. Make sure to register a domain with the .com extension, and if at all possible, pick a name without hyphens (-) and numbers. Additionally, you should set your URL to *yourbandname*.com, but if the domain is already registered, you might have to get a little creative (i.e. add 'band' or 'music' to the domain). I hear it's possible to find cheap domains on GoDaddy. It might be worth a try. Not long ago, I registered an eight-letter domain at Register.com for 99 cents, so it's definitely still possible to find affordable names.

➢ **Set up WordPress:** Bluehost has a one-click install function for WordPress, and it works great.

➢ **Develop a content strategy:** based on the suggestions I made earlier in this chapter, come up with a content strategy that makes sense to you and remember to *write it down*.

➢ **Write a month's worth of posts in advance:** this is something many bloggers or companies do before they

167

ever launch their site. In other words, you can prepare a certain amount of content before you publish your site to the web, and once your blog is set up, you can start scheduling the posts you've pre-crafted. This is likely where you will set your schedule and determine how often you want your blog to populate with new posts. Don't forget to be consistent!

➤ **Create an editorial calendar:** create an editorial calendar for your blogging efforts. Keep a list of blog post titles, add any relevant notes in another column (i.e. I want to write about this subject because I thought of *this*), and create a deadline for yourself. You may even want to add a schedule date and a publish date to your editorial calendar.

12. Podcasting

 New media is like a megaphone. It amplifies your ability to reach more people. - Mark Batterson

Podcasting is a lot of fun. If it weren't, I'm not sure that I would have stuck with it for as long as I have.

From *DAWCast: Music Entrepreneurship* to *Inside Home Recording*, my involvement in the world of podcasts has been varied and diverse. I did several interviews for the *TuneCity Podcast*, I created the *Spark Vinyl Podcast* to promote my home studio, I gave financial advice on the *Amass A Fortune Podcast*, and I have even tried my hand at video game and movie podcasting with the *Scorching Iceberg Podcast* as well as the *AS Movies & Games Podcast*.

You won't necessarily be able to find all of these shows anymore, but at present I still create content for DAWCast: Music Entrepreneurship.

Like a blog, a podcast isn't necessarily a business model unto itself. It can augment and support your marketing efforts, but it won't necessarily be a lucrative proposition out-of-the-box. That isn't to say that there aren't ways of making money with podcasting, however.

Maintaining a podcast tends to require more effort than looking after a blog. Not only does it involve creating audio content, most podcasters also invest significant time into creating show notes, transcriptions, and summaries for each show (which is a good idea). There are definitely advantages to getting into podcasting, but if you want to make it work for you, keep in mind that you will likely need to invest significant effort and time into it.

I'm going to start this chapter by talking about some of the things that I wish I would have considered as I was first getting started in podcasting.

Introduction to Podcasting

I think podcasting is an awesome and engaging form of media. One of the cool aspects of it is that podcast shows don't have to follow a predetermined format like on radio. Podcasters can pick a topic they're interested in and share their own thoughts, opinions and insights in a manner that best suits their style and personality. They can play music on their show (if it's been properly licensed), they can repurpose audio from video content, and they can even syndicate other forms of content like video, PDF or ePub files.

Longer, conversational podcasts have always appealed to me most. I feel like I get more out of longer shows compared to the five to 10 minute shows. I prefer to set my iPod on play and listen for a while as opposed to having to select a new episode every few minutes. I think this is reflected in my own efforts. This isn't to say that show length isn't an important consideration, but if it seems good to you, it will likely seem good to others.

What I didn't immediately realize with podcasting was the fact that it can take a lot of time and effort. There are many activities including editing, production and research, uploading, branding and creating show notes that can feel like quite the time-sink. Additionally, if you choose to do interviews like I have, you'll have to work those into your schedule as well (although that's usually the fun part).

If you're going to make podcasting a part of your online strategy, I would highly recommend marketing it well. All of your time and effort is for naught if nobody hears your show.

When you're first getting started, you won't necessarily have an audience to market your podcast to. You'll have to get your show out there by any means possible (although "Check out my show" and "You should listen to my show" type call-to-actions are not recommended), for all the effort and time you'll be putting in. You might resent any effort that isn't immediately bearing fruit (although I would argue that a long-term mindset is necessary with any project). I always found interviews to be a great way to make my time back, because I would get a lot of great insights from the people I talked to, and I knew expert advice would be value-adding to my audience as well.

Target Market

DAWCast: Music Entrepreneurship has been the longest running podcast I've been a part of (from start to finish). However, I did start it without a clear sense of where it was going or what I wanted to accomplish with it. It just kind of evolved as time went on. That isn't wrong, I suppose, but I think it would have been a good idea to determine the viability of yet another music industry podcast in the iTunes world before even beginning. Would people really want it?

I suppose I had a vague sense of what I wanted to do: I wanted to add value to musicians who were serious about building a career in music. I wanted to expose music industry hopefuls to the various forms of jobs and careers that are available. I wanted to give local artists some exposure.

However, I still didn't give much thought to who my target market would be. I think that makes it a lot harder to know who you should be promoting your podcast to. I wish I had given more thought to that before going and creating loads of content. It may seem obvious, but *when you know who you're after, you'll have an easier time finding them and attracting them.*

So, in summary, think about who your podcast is going to be for. Determine if your podcast idea is in a growth, niche or passion market and find out if there's an audience out there for your work. Ask your existing fans if they would like to consume your content in podcast form. Don't worry about trying to appeal to everyone.

Goals

I think I had some vague ideas about making money and promoting my music and cross-promoting projects... all of which I have done with my podcasts to some degree. However, clearly defined goals would have provided me with specific targets to hit. I didn't really have anything to shoot for when I first got started. I just thought that if I put out enough content, it would eventually get noticed and people would want what I had to offer.

However, with anything – and I can say this with more conviction now than ever before – I think it's important to define your goals. Make them specific. Make them attainable. Set a timeframe and go after them with enthusiasm.

Getting Started

It's not hard to get started in podcasting, especially with audio (video podcasts can take more time and effort than audio podcasts). All you need is a microphone and the means to record sound and you're off to the races.

That's exactly how I got started. I had a headset that I could record my voice with, although I was never quite content with that and started exploring other ways of recording my voice. I upgraded gradually. I had a home studio at the time, so I could have jumped right in and used the best gear I had available, but I wasn't quite comfortable with it yet and moreover, *I just wanted to get started*. That's not a bad mentality to have, mind, and I definitely learned a lot along the way. In hindsight, though, there were a lot of factors I didn't take into consideration.

For one thing, it's good to know the difference between a *condenser mic* and a *dynamic mic*. I knew a little bit about this when I first got started, and I learned more along the way, but unless you're recording in a professional studio or in an acoustically treated room, a dynamic mic is almost certainly the way to go. A condenser mic picks up entirely too much background noise (including reflections and computer fans, which makes it hard to use in proximity to a desktop tower), and it's designed that way. It's meant to pick up the nuances of voice and instruments; that's its function. However, when you're recording voice, especially for a podcast, you don't necessarily need all those finer details in sound. Even in more recent episodes of my podcast, I am guilty of using a condenser mic, mostly because it's the best mic I have, but it was just something I hadn't given a lot of thought to.

Hosting

Something that podcast expert Cliff Ravenscraft recommends is hosting your podcast media files (most likely mp3s) at a separate site as opposed to hosting them on your own site. I am guilty of having done this.

When I first started podcasting, I had my audio files hosted externally, but for whatever reason, the service I was using eventually shut down, so I had to find an alternative. I decided to host the audio on my own site, which eventually led to the decision to create a separate blog and site for the podcast altogether. Many web hosts do say they have enough bandwidth to handle an influx in traffic, but Ravenscraft notes that in many cases, they really don't. If a podcast were to blow up overnight, there are many web hosts that just wouldn't be able to handle that amount of data transfer. If you're not sure, it might be worth checking with your host.

Personally, I use Blubrry to host my podcast episodes. It takes a bit of work to set up (it's pretty easy with WordPress), but it's quite useful and pretty straightforward.

There's quite a bit more that I could get into, but if you're looking to get started in podcasting and you're serious about it, I would recommend checking out Ravenscraft's guides. It's everything I wish I'd known when I got started in podcasting. I am in the process of creating my own guide as well (To access these and other resources, go to: **http://dawcast.com/the-new-music-industry-resource-list/**).

If you'd like to take it a step further, you can also visit the resource page (http://ww.dawcast.com/resources/) on my website.

Format

In the podcasting world, you really aren't limited by a particular format. In the beginning, podcasts were essentially feeds that you could subscribe to in iTunes, and that's more or less where it ended. Today, not only are there more ways of distributing your content, there are also other ways of framing it and presenting it too.

For example, artists like Eminence publish their electronic mixes in podcast form to YouTube. I'm sure that's not the only place they showcase their material, but it seems to be working out pretty well for them.

Podcasting is a medium that is only bound by the audio and video formats. As long as it fits into those mediums, you can do just about anything you want. In fact, you can take an unconventional approach to it if you want to.

I would also recommend looking for different ways of distributing and promoting your podcast. Getting it listed in iTunes might be a worthy endeavour, but that in and of itself may not get it the attention that it deserves. Take your podcast to places where people are likely to listen, whether that's social platforms, forums, video sites or otherwise.

How to Promote Your Podcast and Expand Your Audience

So far, I've talked about some of the errors I've made and some of the important considerations I missed as I was first getting started in the world of podcasting. If you're willing to learn from my mistakes, you can be off to a better start than I was. You will still have to learn as you go, but starting right can help you build greater momentum in the long run.

Here are 25 ways to promote your podcast show and build your audience.

1) **Determine your focus:** people often try to create content that "appeals to everyone", and nowhere is this practice more prevalent than among musicians. Sure, *you* may not know anyone that doesn't like The Beatles, but that doesn't mean that haters don't exist. When it comes to podcasting, a clearly defined niche is power. For example, "music" is far too broad of a subject, but "music that contains hidden messages" is both engaging and specific. You could probably drill even

deeper if you wanted to. When you have the right focus, you can grow your audience faster.

2) **Build your podcast around subjects you are passionate about:** it's a drag to talk about industries and subjects that you have no particular interest in. How will you ever create dozens or even hundreds of podcast episodes around a subject that you're not passionate about? The answer is that you will either *find* a way to be excited about your niche, or you'll quit. The better way to approach it is to start with a subject you can see yourself talking about for a long time to come. You will stick to it for longer if you have enthusiasm for the subject matter, and if you're around for longer, your chances of getting noticed will go up significantly.

3) **Determine your goals:** know *why* you're podcasting in the first place. Is it to grow your fan base? Make money? Build an online community? There isn't a right or wrong answer; there are only answers that are right or wrong for *you*. Create a vision, mission or purpose statement for your show and review it often. Your episodes will begin to take shape around your end goals, making them more effective in the long run. Your purpose should drive your podcast, but if it doesn't, you'll be disappointed when you're not reaching your goal of getting more clients, selling more music, converting more fans, or whatever it may be.

4) **Determine your target audience:** if you want to attract the right people to your content, you will need to

define your target demographic and begin to get into their heads. For example, if you're a freelance writer, your target audience probably isn't thinking, "Gosh, we should really hire a writer", but they *might* be thinking, "I can't believe we fell behind on our blog again. I really wish we had more time to dedicate to it!" Try to identify pain points that you can provide a solution to. People aren't usually thinking in technical terms; they are often thinking in more emotional terms. In short, get into the heads of the people who need what you have to offer. When you know who your target audience is, you can begin to find more people like the ones who have already identified themselves as fans of your work.

5) **Invest more energy into marketing than content:** creating content often takes significant energy, but your efforts will have been in vain if you don't do anything more with it after hitting the 'Publish' button. Cliff Ravenscraft suggests putting 70% of your effort into marketing and building your community and 30% into developing your show. I think that ratio could even be 80/20. I think the human mind has some trouble accepting the importance of promotion because content creation is a *tangible* that feels like work, where marketing and developing connections feels more like an *intangible* that's harder to measure and quantify. While marketing may require a different mindset than content creation, you have to begin to see both elements as a holistic package. Marketing your show is a crucial step you must take to build an audience, period.

6) **Submit your podcast:** your podcast should be discoverable on all of the major platforms and directories. In addition to iTunes, your show should also be submitted to Zune, Blackberry and Stitcher. I would even look into uploading your content to YouTube and SoundCloud, and working towards attracting people on those online communities as well. Where submitting your content to sites like iTunes is a little more of a passive process, uploading your content to a media sharing site like YouTube is more of a proactive process that has to be maintained on an ongoing basis.

7) **Create value-adding content:** if you've figured out your reasons for creating a podcast and who your target audience is, then developing content that resonates with them should prove to be a more natural process. If you've identified potential pain points that they may have and you've found helpful solutions that can serve your audience, then you're well on your way to generating great content. Creating relevant and value-adding content will keep your listeners coming back for more.

8) **Create engaging and entertaining content:** people aren't going to listen to a boring podcast. Many people see it as a form of entertainment, so if you can deliver content that entertains, you are more likely to be successful as a podcaster. Of course, useful, actionable information doesn't hurt either. If your podcast is primarily built on talk, then make sure to exhibit enthusiasm. Podcasts are highly content-driven, so

though production, design, branding and everything else is important, you have to have interesting content to appeal to listeners.

9) **Create positive, uplifting content:** Cliff Ravenscraft notes that there's enough negative out in the world without you adding to it, and I agree. I can't speak for others, but I don't generally listen to podcasts to hear the latest news. I will listen to industry related news, but otherwise, I expect to hear about things that can help me with my work, my marketing, and my life. I bring up the news example, because, media-generated news is pretty aggressively negative most of the time. People find enough negative out in the world. A positive perspective will set you apart.

10) **Convey enthusiasm and passion:** enthusiasm *can* be heard in your tone of voice. We all have off days from time to time, but if you can avoid recording on those days, that would be ideal. If you've started your podcast on a subject you are passionate about, it should come across. Your passion will cause you to stick to it for longer, and it will draw the right people to your show.

11) **Prepare for each episode:** Cliff Ravenscraft says that he prepares for two hours before each show. I can't really tell you how much time you should spend on preparation, because I don't know what your show format is or how long each episode is going to be. However, quality content doesn't just happen on its

own. You have to plan. Be willing to invest as much time as it takes.

12) **Make sure the audio quality is good:** in an audio-centric medium, it serves to reason that audio quality matters. I don't think it necessarily needs to be your top priority, as I have heard many interviews that were recorded over Skype or with a smartphone (I've also recorded interviews this way). It all depends on your interviewee's preferred method of contact. However, if you're recording from home, you have a lot more control over the audio. Go to a quiet room, use a decent quality microphone, and spend a little bit of time editing out extraneous sounds and dead air. Nobody wants to sit and listen to a podcast that hurts their ears.

13) **Build the community:** get to know individuals; not just the community as a whole. Cliff Ravenscraft suggests learning first and last names, and at least one other personal fact about each audience member. Anyone with that kind of determination is sure to do well with the podcasting medium. A personal approach to podcasting brings the community together, and stresses the importance of relationship.

14) **Encourage feedback, especially audio comments:** audio comments are great because you can answer them on your show. Voice messages can be collected using a service like SpeakPipe. The voice of your audience is a valuable asset. Make it a part of your show

so that others can listen in and find out what kind of questions people are asking.

15) **Thank your community:** thank your community members, whether on your show or on social networks. While it is good to send personal messages, you should also thank and acknowledge people publicly whenever possible. Like fans that buy your music, your podcast is only sustained by the people that listen to it.

16) **Build relevant industry relationships:** find other people who are doing what you're doing in the online and podcasting space. Build an ongoing relationship with these people. You could distribute your content to social media and have it ignored, but what would happen if an influencer tweeted about your podcast? It's pretty amazing what can happen when you have the right relationships in place.

17) **Interview people in your industry:** interviews, even with high-profile guests, don't necessarily guarantee a boost in listenership for your podcast. However, if your community is truly engaged in the topic you are covering on your show, they will appreciate interviews with the experts, as they are often value-adding. Not all experts will be open to coming on your show. Make sure to demonstrate a level of commitment to your podcast (i.e. create an archive of content), and if your expert happens to have a new book or product coming out that they want to promote, it's usually an excellent time to do some outreach.

18) **Reciprocate interviews:** be willing to do what your guests do for you. Make appearances on other shows, and prepare to give the best talk you've ever given. Furthermore, always thank guests for their time. Offer to reciprocate with something of equal value. When you appear on other shows, you have the chance to draw a new audience to your show.

19) **Create show notes, summaries, engaging titles and other extras:** if you aren't familiar with basic SEO practices, this would be a good time to get acquainted with them. The tendency might be to simply upload your podcast episode and publish it to your feed. However, if you want to make the most of every episode you create, you should think about adding extras, and you should write up show notes and summaries for your audience too.

20) **Make yourself newsworthy:** being newsworthy is about leveraging the media (TV, radio and print) as a marketing tool. Producers always need new content, because they are constantly under pressure to deliver a story. If you have a great story, the media will be eager to talk to you. If you can position yourself as a trusted expert, producers will even have you back on their programs. This involves finding reporters who cover stories in your niche and developing relationships with them. This can take significant research, but the impact should be obvious. Getting covered through major syndication platforms can drive a lot of traffic to your podcast.

21) **Use social media to market your show:** social media
is for building communities. Assuming that you're doing
the right things here, you should be able to engage
more people with each of your podcast episodes. In
other words, if you've put in the hard work to build your
community, your podcast episodes are simply an
extension of the relationships you've already built.
Social media can also help you to find more people who
are in your target demographic.

22) **Create press releases:** the subject of press releases
was covered in the previous chapter in more detail. You
can gain more publicity for your podcast by finding a
news angle and repurposing the summaries and
descriptions you've already created for each episode.
Press releases can be submitted and distributed for free,
though in general paid services are likely to get better
results. The bottom line here is that not only can you
create a presence for yourself on iTunes; each episode
can then be repurposed and formed into a blog post, a
press release, a video and so forth.

23) **Speak at events where your target audience is:** I
don't have much experience with public speaking yet,
though I have always enjoyed it. I know that many
people fear it, and though it does make me nervous too,
I nevertheless love the experience. Connecting with
your audience from stage is a powerful way to reach
people, because people automatically see you as an
expert when you're the one on stage. For many
marketers, podcasting has led to speaking

engagements at a variety of different events. This is a fantastic way to expand your audience.

24) **Educate your audience:** help them to understand the benefit of podcast subscriptions. Even though podcasts have been around for many years, it seems as though many people still don't know what podcasts are or how they work. Help your audience understand that subscriptions are free, and once they are subscribed, new episodes are automatically downloaded to their audio interface. As a podcaster, the main metric you want to increase is your subscribers.

25) **Build your mailing list:** use your podcast as a platform to build your mailing list. Email is a great way to develop an ongoing relationship with your audience. Furthermore, like a social post, an email can get shared and passed around, extending your potential reach. This is something you should be doing regardless of whether or not you have a podcast.

>> Tools & Tips

To access these and other resources, go to:
http://dawcast.com/the-new-music-industry-resource-list/

> ➤ **How To Grow Your Audience And Market Your Podcast!:** the previous guide was based loosely

on Cliff Ravenscraft's podcast episode on the same subject. I would definitely recommend checking out his guide.

> **Making Yourself Newsworthy:** if the idea of being featured in news piqued your interest, Podcast Answer Man Cliff Ravenscraft also has a show on the subject of being newsworthy. This audio briefly describes how to reach out to the media and features some great tips.

> **How to Start a Podcast - Pat's Complete Step-By-Step Podcasting Tutorial:** Pat Flynn has always had some fantastic things to say about the power of podcasting, and this tutorial is very thorough.

> **SEO: The Free Beginner's Guide From Moz:** for those who'd like to know more about SEO best practices, this is a very detailed guide on how to optimize posts and pages on your website. You don't have to know *that* much to take advantage of SEO tactics, but beginners may want to get educated regardless.

Conclusion

It's important to remember that podcasting - like blogging - isn't necessarily a business model. While it can help you to generate more album sales and website traffic, and you can even get paid for advertising and sponsorships, I have found that it is more of a marketing tool than it is a sales engine. You *can* make money from podcasting, but your initial goal should simply be to engage your fan base.

Because podcasting can take considerable time and effort, it would be better to repurpose and leverage the content you already have; especially as a musician. Otherwise, you might feel like you are always "under the gun" to try to produce weekly or monthly episodes.

If you've recorded a live show, you can use the audio from that show on your podcast. If you've uploaded an acoustic version of one of your songs to YouTube, you can use the audio from that video on your podcast.

This isn't to say that you can't create unique content for your podcast; particularly if you have fewer commitments. Either way, it's a great marketing tool. If you can't see yourself putting a lot of time into it, don't try to do anything too complicated upfront.

>> Tools & Tips

To access these and other resources, go to: **http://dawcast.com/the-new-music-industry-resource-list/**

> **The Future of Podcasting:** in this podcast audio,

I discuss what I see for the future of podcasting and podcast distribution. Though iTunes is the primary distributor of podcasts at the moment, I consider whether or not there's room for competitors to create their own platforms.

➤ **Learn How to Podcast:** Cliff Ravenscraft has an amazing series of free videos explaining how to podcast. Everyone does it a little bit differently, and not everyone uses the same gear, but this is still a fantastic resource if you are new to podcasting.

What I Like

In this section, I'd like to share some of my favourite podcasts with you. While some of them aren't music industry related, I still believe they are all value-adding.

➤ **The Accidental Creative:** the Accidental Creative is aimed at creative professionals who daily work in the create-on-demand world. I have been doing quite a bit of freelance writing in the last year or so, and I have noticed how having to produce content pieces to meet deadlines can put one under a lot of pressure. A musician isn't generally under the gun to produce unless they have a record contract, but there can be many creative pressures and scheduling demands regardless. Todd Henry discusses how creative people can remain prolific, brilliant and healthy. This show features some great interviews as well.

- ➤ **CD Baby DIY Musician Podcast:** if you're an independent artist, this one is a no-brainer. There have been a lot of great interviews on the show that every musician should hear. They usually discuss various news happenings in the industry as well, so if you want to stay up-to-date, you can do so by plugging in to this show. It hasn't seen a lot of updates lately, but the archived content is nevertheless valuable.

- ➤ **The Creative Entrepreneur Podcast:** The Creative Entrepreneur host Bob Baker has been in the music marketing space since the mid 90s. As you can imagine, he is a very experienced and knowledgeable expert in the music industry. These days, he's been doing a series of interviews featuring creative entrepreneurs that make a living in their respective creative fields. The Creative Entrepreneur Podcast is highly recommended for musicians as well, as the mindset that success requires tends to stay pretty consistent from one person to another. Absorbing the thought processes of successful individuals is a worthwhile activity.

- ➤ **Internet Business Mastery:** I've been a long-time listener of Internet Business Mastery, and in addition to internet marketing principles, they have some great mindset tips and book recommendations as well. They also have a community that teaches people how to start their own online business. Of course, if you're a musician, you don't necessarily need to start an internet business on the side. However, if it interests you, these guys do provide great information on the subject.

- ➤ **Music Business Radio:** here's another no-brainer. If you are a musician, you should be listening to the stories of successful musicians on a regular basis. Music Business Radio enables you to do so. And yes, it is available in podcast form. Moreover, host David Hooper also provides valuable music marketing tips and resources over at Music Marketing [dot] com.

- ➤ **The Smart Passive Income Podcast:** I really like what Pat Flynn has been doing with The Smart Passive Income Podcast and the accompanying blog. I feel like this show goes deeper into internet marketing tactics that other podcasters or bloggers simply don't give away for free. This show brought so much of what I already knew about marketing online into sharper focus.

- ➤ **Social Media Marketing Podcast:** if you want to learn how to use social media from the pros, this is a great podcast to listen to. Host Michael Stelzner also has a website/blog called Social Media Examiner that serves as the home to the podcast, and the blog provides equally valuable content.

To access these and other resources, go to:
http://dawcast.com/the-new-music-industry-resource-list/

What I Don't Like

➢ **Editing:** truthfully, there are few things I don't like about podcasting. However, editing can be both time-consuming and labour intensive. Unless you're adequately set up to record a show from start to finish, you will likely have to do some editing afterwards. I used to spend a lot of time on this. Today, I spend significantly less. There are a lot of popular podcasts out there that have not been edited to any great degree. In short, it's not a prerequisite of a great podcast.

➢ **Pressure:** like blogging, being under the gun to produce great content isn't always fun. Keep a running list of ideas in your notebook, or simply keep adding to your editorial calendar. If you've committed to releasing weekly or even monthly podcasts, especially publicly, it's important to deliver for the sake of your audience. Unless extenuating circumstances arise, stay on schedule!

Action Steps

➢ **Purchase the gear you require:** if you want to create a podcast, you need the gear to be able to do it. If you just want to get started, you don't really need more than a computer, a free Digital Audio Workstation and a USB mic. This is all you need if all you want to do is experiment with the medium. However, if you want to podcast like a pro, you're going to have to invest a little more money into equipment. You might look into purchasing a high quality dynamic microphone or broadcast quality microphone, a mixer, a pop shield, a good set of headphones, a digital recorder, software, and other accessories.

- ➤ **Set goals:** think about what you want to accomplish with podcasting. Get as specific as you can. It's a powerful form of media that can lead to other opportunities. However, you can't expect to put in a little bit of effort and reap a harvest of results overnight. Set goals that go beyond the number of shows you intend to produce. It's great to have lots of content, but number goals aren't that hard to reach if you do the work week in and week out consistently. What you really want to figure out is how your podcast is going to benefit others.

- ➤ **Determine your target market:** you need to decide on a tightly defined niche for your podcast. I never much liked it when my college professor said that I would get a better grade on my paper if I wrote on a more specific subject. The problem was that I couldn't figure out how in the world to write a 20 page paper on a topic that I only had two pages worth of information and research on. What I failed to do was consult my professor. He could have given me some guidance and direction. Likewise, because of how small the world is today, you can reach out to other podcasters and ask them about your niche. Other people - especially other experts - can give you a perspective that you probably won't arrive at on your own.

- ➢ **Create a distribution strategy:** your blog can serve as your home to your podcast, but beyond that, how are you going to distribute it? In addition to iTunes, you will likely want to submit it to Zune, Blackberry and Stitcher. You may want to share you content on sites like YouTube (you can create a simple video with a few images) and SoundCloud as well. It's easier to sort this out early on than to try to add channels later. Think about where your audience is most likely to be looking for your content and make sure your podcast can be found there.

- ➢ **Create a marketing strategy:** once you've decided on your goals, your niche, and you have a clear idea on who your target audience is, creating a promotion strategy should prove easier. If nobody hears your podcast, it isn't going to do you much good. Remember to invest more time and energy into marketing and building a community than in producing content.

13. Email Marketing

 Email has an ability many channels don't: creating valuable, personal touches - at scale. - David Newman

If you've already read the other chapters in this book, you're probably starting to get a sense of how important email marketing is.

While this chapter does cover the subject of marketing messages in detail, practically speaking, you will also be using it for your day-to-day communication. You'll be using it to contact venue owners, radio stations, music supervisors and more. As such, you'll want to learn to use it effectively.

What we often forget as a musicians is that communication - be it email or podcasting or social media - exists for the purpose of building relationships. **Marketing** can sometimes put us in the wrong mindset. We think we're supposed to shout from the rooftops about our amazing music, when, in reality, we should be focused on creating value. Email, if used correctly, can be a tool for value creation.

>> Tools & Tips

To access these and other resources, go to:

http://dawcast.com/the-new-music-industry-resource-list/

> ➤ **Why a Marketing Mindset is the Wrong Mindset:** we all know that marketing is a necessary part of a successful music career. However, adopting a marketing mindset can sometimes put you in the wrong frame of mind altogether. This podcast audio explains how to tweak your perspective so that you can approach marketing from the proper frame of reference.

Introduction to Email Marketing

The effectiveness of email marketing is changing very quickly due to some of the micromanaging that Google has been doing. A large number of people use Gmail, and Gmail now organizes email messages into 'tabs'. By default, these tabs are organized into three categories: 'Primary', 'Social' and 'Promotions'. As an aside, you can also create your own tabs if you want to.

So far, most users have been going their merry way without recognizing how their email is being organized by Google. They are not aware that marketing messages (i.e. newsletters that they've opted in for) are now landing in their 'Promotions' tab, which they're not checking.

There are some ways of combating this. You can make your messages more personal in tone, include the user's name in your messages, and cut down on the number of images and links in your campaigns. This will cause more of your emails to show up in the 'Primary' tab in Gmail.

Keep this in mind as you read the remainder of this chapter.

Marketing Messages

Marketing Land conducted a study that showed 77% of people prefer email as the delivery medium for promotional messages. What this means is that your fans prefer to be contacted by email about that new album you just released or that 20-city-tour you're about to embark on, over other methods of communication.

In case you're wondering, social media simply does not compare. There is a video on YouTube that was created by Cyber PR, in which Ariel Hyatt and Jon Ostrow discuss **the dreaded 6%**. What it comes down to is that, on average, only 6% of your fan base will engage with your brand page on Facebook. On an unrelated but still important note, 6% also represents total revenues for independent musicians coming from digital music sales.

While this certainly does not mean you can't market through other channels, it does mean that email is the expected form of delivery for promotional messages. By all means, use your social networks, your blog, your podcast, press releases, postal mail, ads in newspapers and other means to get your news out there.

However, ultimately, if you're planning on sending out a marketing message to your fans, and you want to build a relationship with them, email should be your primary tool of choice.

Email Marketing Tools

An email marketing service is a platform that allows you to create lists of contacts that you can send your marketing messages to. They usually enable you to create opt-in (signup) forms for your website, pick and customize templates, send your messages to segments of your lists, and even set up autoresponders that will automatically send out pre-written messages when certain conditions are met (i.e. when a new user joins your mailing list, a welcome message is automatically delivered to their inbox).

I would advise using an email marketing platform to manage your contact list. I used to send out messages to my list directly from Mozilla Thunderbird or another email client, but ended up having to add and remove names by hand. It was a painstaking process. Not only that, but I couldn't track stats or add much flare to the design of my messages.

Moreover, I would be a little leery about doing something like that these days, as anti-spam legislations continue to get passed.

Email marketing platforms sometimes cost a bit of money (especially as your list increases in size), but the services I'm about to suggest are well worth the price. Subscribers can wilfully unsubscribe from your mailing list without you having to lift a finger. You can track meaningful statistics, like how many people opened your email and how many people clicked on the embedded links. You can customize the design of your email messages to look like your website or brand. You can utilize mobile based designs to cater to your mobile audience. You can set up autoresponders.

MailChimp has some pretty nifty features: it scans your website for the colors you're using by default, and you can also use it to cross-reference your subject line against other similar subject lines that have been used on MailChimp to determine what would be the most effective and engaging title for your campaigns.

My recommended tools for email are Constant Contact, iContact, MailChimp and/or Aweber. They all work slightly differently, and you may even want to use multiple tools depending on the feature-set you require. However, for most people, one tool will suffice. Generally, you can begin by using these services for free, and upgrade to a paid plan at a later date, if necessary.

Tour by Email

In 2012, Chris Robley of CD Baby noted that you could book an entire tour by email. If you read the post, you'll notice that he was somewhat facetious in saying that, but it's not a complete exaggeration (to access this resource, go to: **http://dawcast.com/the-new-music-industry-resource-list/**). If you are confident in your communication skills and know what to say, you could book a lot of shows on the merits of email alone.

This is also highlighted by the fact that many venues now ask for electronic press kits instead of traditional print press kits. It's time-saving and convenient for both ends. Moreover, some venue owners or event coordinators only interact by email and won't book shows by phone, personal contact or any other communication method.

A lot of people still take email pretty seriously, because they know that their followers or user base can't necessarily get in touch with them in any other way. Many solopreneurs, for example, can't really be bothered to answer phone calls all day. Those who have the desire to get in touch with the businessperson will likely use email to correspond, as emails can be dealt with in bulk, in a timely manner.

Email Signature

Think of your email signature as a business card. Every time you send out an email, people will see that signature. More importantly, they will see your name, which will keep you on their radar.

If your email signature is any good, recipients of your email will want to check out your music on your website or come to a show. At the very least, they will see your brand (it can take many impressions for a brand to register with people). Think of how many emails you send out in a year. All of those messages could be plugs for your music (in a non-intrusive, passive kind of way, of course). If you're not doing this already, you are missing out on a valuable marketing opportunity.

Your email signature is a great space to list your website, your tour dates, a press clipping or two, your new album or anything you're currently promoting. If you know a bit of HTML, it's not that hard to include graphical content either. I wouldn't get too carried away in that regard (no animated GIFs please), but check out Amber Rubarth's email signature towards the end of Derek Sivers' article to get a sense of what you could be doing with your email signature (to access this resource, go to: **http://dawcast.com/the-new-music-industry-resource-list/**).

And, just in case we have some newbies reading: most if not all email clients allow you to attach a signature at the bottom of every email you send. Another side benefit of creating an email signature is that it would help you save time from having to type your name and contact information at the bottom of every email message you send out.

Another great way to engage with your signature is to include a photo of yourself. There are many studies showing that faces are known to catch people's attention on the internet, so strategically placing a photo in your email signature (i.e. your eyes are pointed in the direction of your web address and contact information) could be a worthwhile tactic. I have not tried this myself, and I don't think most people expect to see the sender's photo in their signature, but it might be worth experimenting with.

To add a signature in **Mozilla Thunderbird**, you can pull up the "Tools" menu and click on "Account Settings..." Once the Account Settings box pops up, there's a field on the right hand side that allows you to enter your signature. You can also attach a .txt, HTML or image file. If you're not using Thunderbird, you can Google your email client of choice and find applicable tutorials. I know people that swear by Gmail, and I can't say I like it to that degree (not yet anyway), but I do think it's a great tool.

Email Address

For as long as I can remember, I have been trying to sell musicians on the fact that they should have their own website. Yet, many artists continue to use sites like Facebook and ReverbNation as their home on the web.

If that's what you're doing, that's okay. You can do whatever you want. However, if you're serious about your music, you should have a website, plain and simple.

Will a website propel you to stardom? Will it increase your album sales by 500%? Will it get your music in the hands of all of the powerful industry people?

Well, *maybe*. However, that isn't really the point. A tool is nothing more than a tool, and a website is not a magical device that supercharges the growth of your music career automatically. It's not really about the tool itself; it's about what you do with it. A website will almost certainly benefit your online presence, and yes, it may even help you sell more music and connect with A&R reps.

But what's interesting about having your own domain, hosting plan and website is that there tend to be many peripheral benefits that come along with it. Email is one of them. Allow me to explain.

First, answer this question. Which of these two email addresses looks more professional to you?

atomikpenguins@gmail.com

Or...

info@atomikpenguins.com

The point is not whether your band name comes first or last, the point is that, if you have your own website, you can create dozens, if not hundreds of email addresses (it all depends on your hosting plan) ending in @yourbandname.com. You can have chris@yourbandname.com or webmaster@yourbandname.com or tour@yourbandname.com or whatever you want!

In fact, I would *advise* having personalized email addresses with your name(s) in them, because recipients respond better to real people. If they suspect that a bot or a spammer is trying to get in touch with them, they won't be as likely to check your message. So, they may not respond as well to info@yourbandname.com, compared to, say, robert@yourbandname.com.

I'm not saying that Gmail or Hotmail or any other email service is bad. However, if you want to appear professional, a customized email address couldn't hurt. Moreover, you will probably get more traffic to your website, because people will see your email address, become curious, and want to check out what you're about.

Etiquette

Email can be an effective means of communication if used correctly. However, as I've already noted, it isn't about the tool; it's about *how* you use it.

Here are some general etiquette tips for email. These guidelines do not just pertain to email campaigns you send out to your newsletter subscribers. There are times when these principles *don't* apply, but in general email should be used for succinct and concise communication. Remember to get to the point quickly and work on ascertaining the mutual benefit of the interaction. Avoid creating one-way conversations with your recipients.

Here's how to use email with tact.

1) **Think about the desired outcome of the interaction**. In other words, determine the purpose of the communication upfront. Get to the point as quickly as you can.

2) **If the email is a call to action, make sure to outline the benefits for the end-user**. People are generally tuned in to WIIFM ("What's in it for me?") and are not particularly likely to follow through on an offer unless you can provide them with a compelling reason to do so. Both Napoleon Hill and Dale Carnegie would likely advocate personalizing your message, always

remembering to keep the recipient as the central focus of the communication. This is the only way you're going to get the type of response you're hoping for. The same principle also applies to social media.

3) **Make the email easy to answer**. An email containing many questions makes it harder to answer. Too long of a message makes it harder to reply to. Make your emails single-minded in focus and you will have a better response rate. Even if you have many things you wish to ask about, save those questions for another occasion. Create an opportunity for a more focused, in-depth dialogue.

4) **Stick to the facts**. No hype necessary. The temptation as a musician is to oversell who you are and what you do. People tend to see right through that. In many cases, you will find it beneficial to remain humble no matter who you've played with or what you've accomplished.

5) **Establish realism**. You don't dump your entire life story on someone the first time you meet them, do you? Then don't do that with email either! Also, don't shower the recipient with too many compliments. You can complement them if you like; just don't go overboard. It will come across as insincere. Flattery is not a virtue.

6) **Stay relevant**. People are bombarded with spam and various marketing messages all the time. Make sure to mention specific, relevant things in an email, especially

when you're addressing someone personally (i.e. "Hi David! I heard episode 32 of your podcast and absolutely loved what David Hooper had to say about postal mail!"). I'll be honest; I tend to ignore emails that don't begin in this manner.

7) **Use a signature**. Study the previous section to create a unique, engaging email signature for yourself.

12 Effective Email Marketing Strategies

There is more to the art of email marketing than you may even realize. Because this method of communication has been in use for a long time, marketers have had the chance to collect vital statistics and analyze the results. Therefore, there is a lot of useful data out there that can be used to create better campaigns. You will find some of that data in the following points.

1) **Personalize your messages:** there used to be a time when addressing people by name was the accepted norm with email campaigns. Most email marketing platforms allow you to store the first names of your users and later "call" it with a line of code. Though personalization is certainly one of the keys to success with email, you don't necessarily want to use names anymore, as some people are concerned about hacking and identity theft. Having said that, there are a variety of ways to personalize your emails. You can customize who the email is coming from, and as you might imagine, a person's name is often more engaging than a

brand name (I started using my name in my emails instead of my website's name and my open rate jumped up by about 5%). You can personalize the message of your email effectively by imagining what it would be like to be on the receiving end of your communication and writing in such a way that relates and connects.

2) **Craft a subject line:** arguably, the subject line of your email is more important than any other element. If you write an effective subject line, more people will open your email. If not, all of the work you put into crafting the message could end up being a waste of time. According to Buffer, subject lines with 60 to 70 characters should be avoided (that's 60 to 70 **characters**; not 60 to 70 words). 70 characters and up is okay, and fewer than 49 also tested well. You can also experiment with shorter subject lines (one or two words), which are trending right now.

3) **Time your messages:** in other words, you need to send out your marketing messages strategically. It won't do you much good to send them out randomly, whenever you feel like it. For a long time, the purported best practice was to send out messages between Tuesday and Thursday, from about 10 AM to 12 PM Eastern Time, and a lot of marketers still do. I have had some success with that. However, Buffer notes that the timeframe from 8 PM to midnight is ideal. Theoretically, there are fewer marketers sending out their messages between those hours. Feel free to experiment a little, especially while you still have a smaller mailing list.

4) **Give away freebies:** people love free tools, templates and giveaways. As a musician, you may want to give away mp3s of live performances, jam sessions, acoustic reinterpretations of your songs, or even CDs and other merch. However, one of the best things you can do is direct people to your website where they can download a digital file, because, that will allow you to "touch" them a second time. You can send them to a landing page (with nothing but the download link on it), and have them 'like' your band on Facebook or send them to buy your album on iTunes as well. You can create any kind of additional call to action you want below the download link.

5) **Be mobile friendly:** most if not all email marketing platforms have built-in templates and options for mobile users. According to Buffer, 47% of all emails are opened on mobile devices today. This means that you should be taking measures to meet this growing demand. Don't forget; you don't have to have the prettiest email messages in order to engage. You just need great content. You should also separate important links in your email from other links and text, as it can be challenging to tap on a link on a mobile device if it is crowded out by other content. Additionally, it was once thought that HTML messages would overtake standard text messages, but you'll be surprised by the number of marketers that still use predominantly text-based messages to reach out to their audience. I have used both types of messages, and though both formats have worked well for me, the one thing that ended up failing

was when I temporarily went from graphical messages back to a text-only email. The open rate on that email dropped to about 1%. So, once you've decided on a format, it may be a good idea to stick with it.

6) **Re-engage inactive users:** one of the realities of email campaigns is that an open rate of 15 - 20% is considered average and even good. What you're going to discover, of course, is that your emails are going to be ignored by a certain number of people on your mailing list (Buffer notes that the average is 63%). Some marketers recommend purging these inactive users from your list entirely, as there is no need to communicate with people that don't care about your marketing messages. You can also increase your open rates by doing this. However, before you do that, you might want to give those users one last chance to stay on your list. Send a campaign that's specifically tailored to those people. For example, you might send an email with the subject line, "We're sorry to see you go...", "We wish you would come back", or something similarly attention-grabbing. If they let you know that they would like to receive future communication from you, don't scrub them from your list. Otherwise, purge mercilessly.

7) **Tell a story:** storytelling is perhaps one of the most powerful marketing tools to incorporate in your messaging toolbox. When stated that way, it might sound a little slimy or manipulative, but the reality is that people *always* want to know the **why** behind a decision more than they want to know the **what**. Not

only does storytelling make good marketing sense, it actually serves to build a better connection with your audience too.

8) **Build a positive reputation:** if you have a good reputation, more people will open your emails. If you want to build a positive reputation, make sure to keep your promises, deliver the goods, and try to answer any questions community members may have. For example, if you had a show on Saturday and you promised your audience that the photos for that show would be up on your website by Tuesday; make sure that the photos are actually available for them to view by the promised time.

9) **Focus on the content:** it might seem like a good idea to have awesome looking emails. However, like I was saying earlier, the reality is that people tend to care more about the content than the design. This does not mean that you shouldn't put any effort into making your emails look attractive, but readers tend to get distracted by too many visuals onscreen. Write compelling copy, and your subscribers will respond more to that. Limit the options in your emails and only provide calls to action that you actually want your reader to follow through on.

10) **Segment your lists:** your mailing list is probably made up of a variety of different people; local fans, at-a-distance fans, online or worldwide followers, social media followers, and so forth. None of this is of any use to you and your email campaigns unless you've slotted

these people into disparate, segmented lists. This can seem pretty tedious, but your emails will be far more effective when your opt-in list is organized into meaningful segmentations. You have to decide how you want to split people up. For example, if touring is a priority to you, you might want to break up your list into different localities. When you make it a point to contact people with something they already *want* to know, their response will surprise you.

11) **Make it timely and relevant:** relevant, timely and controversial is the name of the game when it comes to content, whether you're writing blog posts or emails. Not only that, but if you make it a habit to send your users relevant information, your emails will appear less spammy. Thus, you will minimize unsubscribe rates.

12) **Create calls to action:** you aren't just sending out emails for the heck of it, right? All of your messages should contain a) a purpose, and b) a call to action. A call to action is something for your subscribers to do. Just as an example, you might have a button that says, "read more", "buy now", "download now", "attend", or something to that effect. When the purpose of your communication is clear, it's easy to direct your community members to do what you want them to do.

>> Tools & Tips

To access these and other resources, go to:
http://dawcast.com/the-new-music-industry-resource-list/

> ➤ **8 Effective Email Marketing Strategies, Backed by Science:** I referenced this article a couple of times in this list, so I thought I should link it up. It's a great article with a lot of useful information.

Conclusion

In general, as a marketing platform, email is thought to be more important than even social media; and believe me, I've written a monster chapter on the subject of social media. Used right, social media has massive potential. However, if you find yourself in a situation where you have to choose between one and the other, I would recommend building your mailing list first. Moreover, many of the popular email management tools allow you to cross-post to social media as well, letting you hit two birds with one stone.

Like text messages, emails can be ignored or looked at later. In other words, you can "touch" your fans directly with your emails without being too intrusive. Additionally, unless people delete your messages, they remain in their archives. If they ever have a need to contact you, or they come across an opportunity that seems right for you, they can quickly search up one of your marketing messages and get in touch with you (and that's something that can't be done quite as easily with text).

What I Like

> **Ease of use:** let's face it; when the phone weighs like a brick, it's much easier to send an email than to make a call. That isn't to say that you shouldn't call people, especially when you've already made arrangements to do so, but a lot of people still take email seriously, so you have that working in your favour. Even podcast interviews can be arranged by email, so you're not a lost cause if all you can get yourself to do is contact people by email.

> **MailChimp:** at one point or another, I started using MailChimp for all of my email marketing efforts. Previous to this, I had been using several different services to send out campaigns and manage my lists. I was a little resistant to streamlining at first, because I used to be in charge of sending out promotional messages for a certain music company, and we always used MailChimp. Suffice to say, we experienced some frustration with tweaking templates and getting our lists set up. However, over the long haul, it worked out fairly well. MailChimp has some easy-to-use mobile templates, and even their free software is quite good. Most if not all email management tools have paid programs as well, but if you want to start free, I don't know that there's anything that compares to MailChimp.

What I Don't Like

➢ **Crafting marketing messages:** like exercise, while I don't necessarily enjoy crafting emails, I like the benefits of it, and how it allows me to build an ongoing relationship with my community. That is more or less my mindset around email marketing. It takes up time in my schedule that I would happily spend elsewhere. However, list growth does cause you to be more grateful for the medium. Ultimately, crafting marketing messages isn't *that* bad.

➢ **Clutter:** clutter is perhaps the worst aspect of email. Over time, you end up having to create numerous email accounts, and while I have found that you can manage all of your messages from a single inbox, sometimes there is good reason to have separate accounts for different purposes. Even if not for that, over time, you wind up on a variety of mailing lists, so your spam and junk pile keeps growing. Unless you are particularly diligent, it's hard to keep your inboxes neat and organized.

➢ **Lack of productivity:** author and speaker Brendon Burchard has noted that email is essentially a convenient organization system for other people's agendas. When you *really* think about it, it's true. It shouldn't be a high priority activity, even for a musician. Communication is necessary, of course, but the messages you receive are generally what others have in mind for you. Email isn't wrong. What's wrong about it is that it puts you in the wrong mindset. Your day should not begin with other people's agendas for you. It should begin with *your* agenda for you.

Action Steps

- **Create an account with an email marketing service:** find an email marketing platform that you like, and create an account with them. If you are just beginning to build your list, a free option will likely do everything you need it to do for now. If you have a larger list, it may be necessary to explore paid options. Some of the most popular email marketing tools include: AWeber, Constant Contact, iContact and MailChimp.

- **Place opt-in forms on your website:** this is a no-brainer. Once you've created an account with a site like MailChimp or iContact, you can start growing your mailing list on your website immediately. The best way to entice people to opt-in for your mailing list on your website is to offer something for free (i.e. "If you sign up for our mailing list, we'll send you a free MP3 off of our new album!"). You should also strategically place call to actions on your website to encourage visitors to join. You might place these opt-in forms at the end of your blog posts, or below your bio. Figure out which pages people are visiting most, and place your offers there (if not on *every* page).

- **Place opt-in forms on your social media profiles:** you may not be able to do this with every social profile, but on a Facebook page, for example, you can install an app called 'Static HTML' and create a landing page where you can have your visitors subscribe to your newsletter. On Twitter, you could simply share a link to a landing page on your website enticing people to sign up.

➤ **Collect email addresses at your shows:** you have the opportunity to collect email addresses at every show you play. While you may have some success with a sign-up sheet at the back of the venue, there are a variety of other options you can explore these days. For example, you could pass around an iPad from the stage and have people sign up electronically. You could have a laptop at the merch table and do the same. You could have people scan a QR code on their smartphones. Whatever the case, try to create a value proposition to entice people to want to sign up. Offer something for free, or take a picture of the audience and tell them that you're going to post it on your blog the following day. Tell them that you're going to send them an email and let them know when the pictures are going to go live.

➤ **Create autoresponders:** you can automate commutation with your mailing list subscribers by setting up autoresponders. For example, you can welcome your newcomers one week, send them a survey the following week, send them to a download link the next, and so on. Autoresponders don't negate the need for regular communication with your fans, especially if you want to let them know about your upcoming show or music release, but they do allow you to "fill the gaps" in your communication without having to log in to create a new message every week or every couple of weeks. You will still have to create these messages individually, of course.

14. Social Media

> ❝ Too many brands treat social media as a one-way broadcast channel rather than a two-way dialogue through which emotional storytelling can be transferred. - Simon Mainwaring

It's amazing how many bands and artists miss the point of social media.

Check us out on YouTube. Come to our show on Friday. Buy our new album. Vote for us.

There's a time and a place for a well-placed call to action, and at times "check out _____" is the right thing to say. However, most musicians would do well to remove it from their vocabulary altogether.

If you want to engage, you have to ask yourself what people are going to be drawn to. For example, consider these two messages:

"Buy our latest album. It's awesome!"

And...

"The intro to our latest single features the voice of someone famous. You'll never guess who."

I don't know about you, but I wouldn't follow through on the first message; especially if it was a band I didn't know. The second message would *at least* get me to check out the tune.

This is marketing 101. A lot of your marketing will be far more effective if you first ask the question, "How do I draw people in?"

The truth of the matter is that you already make many decisions in your daily life based on marketing, whether you are aware of it or not. This is important to know, because marketing means *influence*. Once you learn to tune in to *how* businesses are advertising their products and services, you will begin to see that the same tactics continue to be used and repurposed over and over again.

Over time, I've come to recognize when I've been sucked in by good marketing, and I *still* eat it up. Human nature is human nature. If you understand basic psychology, it's not hard to decode why certain advertising works so well.

Why do so many bands continue to spam their followers with "buy this", "do that", "come here", and "vote for us"? It could be due to a poor understanding of marketing, but it is more likely due to *laziness*.

You see, it requires a lot of thought and planning to craft an interesting story and core message. If you wanted to include the voice of a famous person in a song, you might have to go through the correct channels to license it. You might have to wait for clearance to use their voice. You might have to build the intro of the song around their voice. I think you get the picture.

In other words, you have to *start with an interesting idea*. Does this sound like too much work? Well, if you want your message to really connect with your followers, you have to see things from their perspective.

You also have to remember that call-to-actions aren't particularly value-adding. They should still be a part of your messaging, but they shouldn't be the permanent fixture of your status updates.

Always try to imagine being on the receiving end of your communication. Would *you* click on that link or button? Would *you* buy your album? Would *you* vote for you? Why or why not?

If your message is interesting, you will also stand out from the competition, because, more than likely, *they* are still posting: "check us out".

Introduction to Social Media

Social media is transient by nature. As you can imagine, the information I present here could be obsolete in a very short period of time. However, I do believe that social media will remain relevant in the years to come, and is a subject that has to be covered. Utilizing social platforms is a necessary part of music marketing.

I will try to provide you with the right mindset so that you can succeed in social media, regardless of how it changes.

Keep Informed

Are you aware of the latest trends in the world of social media? Are you watching the rankings? Do you know about the different ways you can use different sites to promote your content?

Though keeping informed does not have to be high on your priority list, it still needs to be there.

Here are two things you should be doing:

1) Reading at least two articles or listening to one podcast episode on the effective usage of social media every week.
2) Checking to see what the most popular social media sites are every month or two.

For point 1, I personally subscribe to Social Media Examiner to keep up-to-date with the social media world. Sometimes I will read half a dozen or more blog posts on the subject in a day. Am I suggesting you do the same? No.

The social media rules and climate changes frequently (just look at all the unwelcome design changes Facebook has brought us without much prior notice). One day your posts are reaching many of your fans. The next day you have to pay to reach more people. It may seem silly, but it has happened before and it *will* happen again.

Another good reason to read up on social media is so that you can learn from people who've actually had some success with it.

I would suggest using eBizMBA for point 2. You can also type in "Top 15 Most Popular Social Networking Sites" or something to that effect in Google and the first result should be the eBizMBA rankings.

The main purpose of this activity is to keep track of where the most users are. When MySpace took a nose dive back in 2007/2008, many of its users widely adopted Facebook in exchange. As a musician, you don't really want to be left out of sudden shifts like that. You have to go to where the people are. Social media is going to continue to evolve and you need to be on the watch. If Facebook were to begin a downward spiral tomorrow and people started using a different site, you might want to get a move on that new platform.

MySpace was, and still is, a pretty good place for music. In fact, the **New Myspace** was unveiled earlier in 2013. However, up until recently, MySpace had looked like a musical graveyard. Many bands hadn't updated their profile since 2007. That's fine, but if it were me and I wasn't planning on updating it again, I would consider deleting my profile altogether because I wouldn't really want it popping up in a Google search (I've done new things since 2007, thank you very much).

Frequent Engagement

Consistency is important, even with social media.

Status updates can become outdated very quickly. Not only that, but if you don't post often, it will look as though you never use your profile to interact with your followers.

Do you have to post to your pages and profiles every single day? Maybe not if you're an established entity, but if you're still working on building loyal followers who frequently engage with your content, it wouldn't be such a bad idea. Some well-established people post three or four times per week, if not three to four times per day!

The great thing about social media is that each new post can be an experiment. Sites like Facebook do a great job of logging analytics, so you can track which posts are engaging. If you find something that works, keep doing that. If something isn't working, you could always tweak it or try something else. You have no reputation to tarnish when you're first getting started.

Much like blogging, frequent posting can be accomplished through scheduling posts in advance. You don't have to be on Facebook or Twitter every day if you don't want to, but you will want to 'like' the comments people leave and respond to them when appropriate. This brings me to my next point.

Third Party Tools

In some cases, you may find it helpful to use third party tools to manage your various social media accounts. Personally, I like to schedule some of my content in advance so I don't have to check in every day (especially on Twitter). For that purpose, I like to use:

HootSuite: HootSuite allows you to schedule your tweets and posts well in advance of them ever being seen by your followers. You could take some time to plan out what you want your tweets to say for the next month (or more) and have them automatically pushed out at a time of your choosing. In other words, you can bulk-task, which I find to be a time saver.

With HootSuite, you can also manage your Facebook, Google+, LinkedIn, foursquare, MySpace and mixi accounts as well as your WordPress blog natively. If you want to stay with the free version, however, you can only manage up to five accounts at a time, so choose wisely.

Buffer: a lot of people love Buffer, but it took me quite a while to figure out why. Essentially, you can use the platform to have social media posts pushed at optimal times of the day. Buffer also provides you with new suggestions ever so often, so that you don't have to go looking for interesting things to post. This is a great tool for keeping your social "buffer" topped up. You can connect your account with Twitter, Facebook, LinkedIn, Google+ and App.net.

TweetDeck: this is a great tool for managing multiple Twitter accounts. It displays @mentions, private messages, and your 'following' stream. You can also arrange your feeds in customizable columns. Much like HootSuite, you can schedule tweets as well (but only tweets). TweetDeck also alerts you of new tweets, direct messages and mentions.

Other: there are a variety of other social tools, plugins and platforms available to you. You can have your blog posts fed over to Facebook or Twitter. You can have your Facebook and Google+ posts fed over to Twitter. You can have your Instagram photos cross-posted to Twitter, Facebook and your blog. This can make your social media efforts more streamlined, although it can't hurt to post some unique content on each social platform as opposed to just recycling the same content across all platforms (you can also re-purpose the same content using different headlines and pictures, especially if a post didn't engage the way you hoped it would the first time around).

To access these and other resources, go to: **http://dawcast.com/the-new-music-industry-resource-list/**

Facebook

Facebook is the most popular social networking site today. That also means it's the most saturated. You won't find too many bands that haven't moved over from MySpace, not to mention new bands that weren't around when MySpace was still popular. Your goal as a musician should always be to create genuine fans whether that involves social media or not. This will guarantee an audience who actually cares about what you have to say on your Facebook page. When you really think about it, it's kind of like reverse engineering.

You've probably heard before that video is one of the most engaging forms of content. However, on social media, it seems people engage with photos just as much, if not more. Therefore, when putting together your Facebook strategy, you should be thinking about using photos often. In a way, it makes sense. When you see in your feed that someone commented on or liked so-and-so's photo, you can't help but click on it and see it for yourself.

Take some time to get to know what people are actually engaging with on Facebook (and social media in general) before you go asking for people to come to your show or buy your album. I wish I would have done this, because I only posted to Facebook haphazardly when I felt I actually had something to talk about. You will find that some of the most followed people post pretty frequently (although there are always exceptions).

Some marketers advise keeping the ratio of your call-to-actions to 4:1. In other words, only post one marketing centered message for every four engagement posts. Some say the ratio should be 20:1, and some would even have it at 40:1. Fundamentally, regardless of how you choose to do it, remember to engage more often than you sell and you should do well.

For example, George Takei has over eight million 'likes' on Facebook (as of February 2015), and that isn't just because he was on the original Star Trek TV series. It's because he's constantly posting funny pictures and videos and adding his own comments and personality to them. Guy Kawasaki also does something similar, except he does it on Google+. Take note of people who are popular on social media. What can you learn from them? How could you apply their techniques to your own social media strategy?

Twitter

Surprise, Twitter is the second most popular social networking site today. This probably doesn't come as a shock, but what you may not know is that Twitter has been evolving.

For one thing, your Twitter profile page is more customizable than ever. You can upload a customized background (which you will probably want to look into), pick colors, and you can also use a customized header image. In other words, branding your Twitter page has never been easier. You can utilize your background and branding to direct more traffic to your website or other social media profiles from your Twitter page.

Another thing you should be aware of is that Twitter is *also* going photo heavy, as you can now attach media content to your tweets. Again I would recommend engaging with photos and other media on Twitter, though it's perfectly okay to tweet out text-based posts too.

Twitter has gradually been removing their API and support for various third party tools. As result, most auto-following or auto-unfollowing apps are no longer supported.

LinkedIn

LinkedIn is the third most popular social networking site on the internet right now, and has been a bit of a moving target. Not long ago, they gave the interface a facelift, and it definitely feels more social oriented than before. In fact, LinkedIn has been making changes to their site and adding new features just about every month. However, it's still geared towards professionals.

The other reason it's a moving target is because it has been debated as to whether or not it has any practical value for musicians. The short answer is that *it does*. Is it a required platform? Should every musician have a LinkedIn profile? Probably not.

You have to keep in mind that every social networking platform takes time to learn. Facebook took you some time to set up. You probably don't remember it, but I assure you it did. It will be the same for LinkedIn, should you choose to make it part of your social media marketing package. Be careful not to use that as an excuse, because when new social networking sites come along, you will have to go through the same process. Furthermore, I don't think it's a matter of *if* but *when*.

The best way to connect on LinkedIn is with groups. There are many groups that have been created with musicians, singers, songwriters and producers in mind. You can connect locally and globally. Much like Facebook, depending on how you have your notification settings set up, you can receive emails letting you know when people have added to current discussions in groups. This can help you keep track of the conversations. You can also start your own group if you're so inclined.

Since LinkedIn is largely a professional space, you'll want to keep your conduct professional. Ask questions and answer questions. Approach discussions from the perspective of what value you can add to participants. This will ultimately help you create new contacts, which is one of the most valuable resources you can generate.

You can also post updates to your followers just like you would on any other social networking site. You could use a tool like HootSuite to schedule posts to roll out on LinkedIn as well.

Pinterest

Pinterest is one of the fastest growing social platforms, and it has continued to rise through the ranks to fourth place. Here's what you need to know about Pinterest: it was the fastest to the 10 million user mark over any other social networking site, and *it's driving the most referral traffic* of any social platform right now.

What this means is that people are getting more hits and visits to their websites and blogs from Pinterest over any other social media site. So, not taking advantage of it, especially if you're a visually heavy band, seems kind of silly.

With that in mind, Pinterest isn't intended for reckless self-promotion. Like LinkedIn, it's best to approach it with a bit of tact. Pinterest is essentially a digital scrapbook, a place for 'pinning' all of the beautiful and wonderful things you find on the internet. The best practice here is to create various 'pinboards' and categorize the content you 'pin' (photos and videos). For example, you could create boards for "Band Photos", "Head Shots", "Album Artwork", "Live Performance Videos", etc.

I know, you might feel a little silly doing it, but if Keith Urban and Lady Antebellum can make it work for them, you can probably find a way to engage on Pinterest too. Is it absolutely required? No. But if you have a strong visual element to your music, you may want to look into it.

Make sure that your pins link back to your website, your blog posts or social profiles. Pinning a photo is great, but having it link back to other pieces of content is even better.

Google+

Google+ is currently the fifth most popular social networking site on the internet with approximately 500 million users.

At first, I wasn't excited about Google+ at all. When it was still in the early stages of development, it seemed like it could potentially be a good tool for music promotion, under-crowded as it was.

Unfortunately, I gave up. I shouldn't have. I just found the interface hard to comprehend at first. Daria Musk was in a similar position and actually became known globally overnight utilizing Google+ Hangouts (that's really rare, by the way). I'm not saying that this would have happened to me, mind you. She was clearly better prepared and better positioned for it.

Then I came back to Google+ when I was developing a social media strategy for TuneCity. It took me awhile, but I started figuring it out and actually got excited about it. At first, I wasn't sure why, but this is what I started to realize:

1) **Google+ has a clean and simple interface**: Google+ is uncluttered compared to a lot of social networking sites. It has gone through a few facelifts, and the platform is sleeker, and more visually oriented than before, but it's still simple.

2) **Google+ boasts good blog connectivity (authorship):** you can list yourself as a contributor to the blogs you write on and backlink using the rel=author tag.

3) **Google+ circles are awesome**: circles make it easy for you to categorize the people in your network. On Facebook, *by default*, all of your connections get lumped in as "Friends". With Google+, you can create your own "circles" and make categories that will actually help you later remember who does what (i.e. "Fans", "Session Musicians", "Promoters", "Booking Agents", etc.). At the moment, you can circle anyone and everyone, which makes it a little bit like the old MySpace.

4) **Google+ events are awesome**: Google+ events have a lot of cool features, but integration with Google Calendar was the only convincing I needed. In my opinion, the functionality is far better than what Facebook offers. Plus, people don't really check Facebook events anymore.

5) **Google+ doesn't display any ads**: Google+ doesn't display any ads as of this writing. This keeps the interface uncluttered. And, frankly I wouldn't mind seeing a few AdSense ads on there (but that's probably just me). The interface *is* a little busier than before, so it's probably a good thing.

Of course, because it's a Google platform it's also good for search. This may or may not remain an advantage, but for now posting keyword rich content can get you discovered in search results. I am often surprised to see some of my Google+ posts showing up in search results pages.

Tumblr

Tumblr is a Web 2.0 social networking site that allows users to post content in blog form. Some artists, like Pomplamoose or Macklemore & Ryan Lewis actually use Tumblr to populate the blog feed on their website. I wouldn't be too quick to do this, as you never know when the site could go down, but there's nothing saying you can't.

Some social networks, like Instagram, allow you to cross-post to Tumblr. In other words, you *could* engage on Tumblr without ever creating unique content for it. You can also use the Jetpack plugin in WordPress to connect to your Tumblr account, so whenever you have a new blog post, you can have it pushed to Tumblr and other sites.

Typically, some of the most engaging blogs on the platform are those that feature photo content with some text. In other words, it's a great place for a photo blog.

Another way to take advantage of it is to create links to your website and other social platforms. You could do quick write-ups that also include links to places you want to send your visitors to.

The demographic on Tumblr is pretty young, and there are a lot of people following musicians, so it seems like a good place to be for a band.

Instagram

I've already talked quite a bit about engaging with photos, and here's a tool that's tailor made for this purpose. Instagram is a photo sharing smartphone app that has adopted many of the conventions (likes, @mentions and #hashtags) of other popular social platforms. It also connects with Facebook, Foursquare, Flickr, Posterous, Tumblr and Twitter. If you're using a WordPress blog, you can use a plugin to have your photos displayed on your site.

Here's a tip if you are in a band: create a band profile that everyone has access to. It may take a little bit of coordination (you may want to avoid everyone posting at once), but you'll be able to share in the responsibility of generating interesting content from different perspectives. You can still create individual profiles too, if you want to.

Another tip is to create and organize photo themes with #hashtags. Similar to blogging, you may find it helpful to snap shots of specific things like sunsets, trees, guitars or anything else that could make for engaging subject matter. This is a good way to get un-stuck creatively.

MySpace

Oh yes, MySpace. When I was beginning work on this book, it was *still* the fifth most popular social networking site on the internet. It has dropped off the list as sites like Tumblr, Instagram and Vine gain in popularity, but MySpace isn't completely irrelevant.

Huh?

Yeah, I was surprised too. Even in this post-Facebook world, MySpace is showing some signs of life. Don't get me wrong; they're still bleeding money, and while the site interface has been updated, it just hasn't completely resonated with their user base. However, it still has a chance to catch on again.

People gave dozens of reasons for leaving MySpace in 2007/2008. The ugly interface. The slowdowns. The ads. The learning curve.

In 2013, the New Myspace launched. It seems to run a lot smoother than before, and it definitely looks sleeker. Previously, the focus was on individual profiles, but now, as predicted, search and discovery appears to be a greater emphasis. The new platform allows you to share your updates to Facebook and Twitter, which is a welcome addition.

There are rumours going around that Myspace is beginning to delete profiles. I have not confirmed that phenomenon as of yet, but if that is the case, it could be as projected: they are moving towards mainstream media. Even if not for that, you will have to search for anything that wouldn't be considered mainstream, because the landing page used to have Justin Timberlake on it, and the front panel featured headlining artists like Beyoncé. If there's anything good to say about it, it would be that it's putting music at the center again.

Indeed, music is the main focus of the new Myspace. There is good reason to keep tabs on it as a musician.

Bandcamp & Music Distribution

Until recently, Bandcamp didn't really have a social component at all. However, this popular music distribution site has been evolving to include more social functions, and when they began integrating the social networking aspect, their sales jumped by 40%.

The popularity of Bandcamp, as far as I can see, is based on a few things:

1) The ability to sell music at a price you set.

2) Fewer middlemen taking a cut.

3) The popularity of digital sales, which goes hand in hand with point 2 (some musicians don't like giants like iTunes and Amazon taking a cut).

4) Easily customizable pages.

Some musicians even use Bandcamp as their personal website. There are reasons why I wouldn't recommend that, but that goes for any social networking site. I wouldn't use any of the platforms mentioned here as a personal website.

Personally, I have no problem with a company taking a cut if they can deliver results. CD sales at CD Baby have actually gone up in the last few years. They are very good at moving merchandise. If I were more proactive about selling my music, I would leave the *selling* part to a company like CD Baby (I do anyway), especially if I didn't have a track record of moving product or selling digital music through my own website (which I don't). I believe in utilizing the strengths of other services, not reinventing the wheel.

It's too easy to think in terms of *scarcity*. CD Baby is not evil. iTunes is not evil. Bandcamp is not *less* evil than the alternatives. They are all tools.

A lot of musicians I've talked to seem to be concerned about distribution. I don't really understand why, because distribution - at least *digital distribution* - has never been easier. Pay out a couple of 20s and you can have a company like CD Baby or TuneCore get your music on iTunes, Amazon, and a variety of other stores and streaming sites. Sure, you don't have control over what percentage of money you make, but my feeling is that digital sales are a *supplemental income*, not a *primary income*. It's a bonus on top of physical sales, merch sales, live performance, and other income streams. If you don't have other sources of income, you probably don't have a music *career* yet.

How to Develop a Successful Social Media Strategy

Social media is sometimes narrowly defined to encompass little more than social networks like Facebook or Twitter. However, when you really think about it, it is interconnected with a variety of other online components. It has a fairly symbiotic relationship with blog posts (because they can be shared with social share buttons) as well as email. In short, developing a successful social media strategy isn't just about the social networks you use; it's about bringing all of your online marketing efforts into synergy.

Here's how to put together an effective social strategy:

- **Outline your goals:** social media engagement can be haphazard if you don't take the time to set goals. Frequent engagement might be a worthy goal, but you may also find it beneficial to orient your marketing around clearly defined campaigns. For example, if you have a new album coming out, you should start teasing people before it is ever released and long after it comes out. If you have a plan in place, this will prove much easier to execute.

- **Develop a plan:** a great way to develop a social media strategy is to **mind map**. Mind maps are visual diagrams that are considered to better reflect the way a person thinks (and the way your brain works), especially compared to the linear nature of lists. Because of all of the social networks that are available, it can be worthwhile to create a spider diagram and categorize each site and understand how they connect.

- **Build your mailing list:** at first glance, it may seem as though your mailing list has nothing to do with social media. However, if you aren't using your email list to generate more followers, you're doing something wrong. Moreover, the two platforms tend to compliment each other very well. Your email marketing messages can be shared to social media, and social platforms can be used to entice more people to opt-in for your newsletter.

- **Develop focus:** social media campaigns are less effective when you don't have a goal and a focus in mind. While "engagement" is always a good aim to have, if it's not guided by a target, your efforts will often "end" without reaching any specific destination. Think of it this way. When you are preparing for a show, you follow a specific process. You may not have documented procedures for what you do (I would recommend doing this, as it would ultimately make you more efficient), but there is a progression that you follow. It might start with booking the show. Then, once the show is booked, you begin rehearsing. You also initiate marketing campaigns to let your fans know about the upcoming show. Then you pack up your gear the day of the show or the night before. Then you set up your gear at the venue and sound check. This is a fairly simplistic overview of everything that goes into preparing for a performance, but it all happens because you have an objective in mind. You *built up* to the show. Similarly, if you want to maximize the effectiveness of your social media campaigns, you will want to build up to something. Tease people. Chronicle your journey. Tell stories. Ramp up to the release of an album or a national tour.

- **Initiate crowdfunding campaigns:** artists like Amanda Palmer and Jack Conte speak highly of crowdfunding campaigns, and for good reason. Notwithstanding, from everything that I've seen and read, I would be inclined to believe that crowdfunding initiatives require great focus and determination. Fortunately, there is plenty of room to make mistakes without incurring major consequences. For example, if your Kickstarter campaign isn't successful, you don't get to keep any of the funds. However, the lessons you learn from promoting a project of this nature allow you to build towards a more successful campaign in the future. Furthermore, a crowdfunding campaign is an excuse to engage everyone you know and ask them to spread the word. A well-promoted proposal will gain the attention of more people, which will also lead to more followers for your social profiles. If you want to explore crowdfunding further, there are a variety of resources that can be found on YouTube as well as across the web.

- **Leverage and re-purpose your content:** if you aren't re-purposing your content in a variety of different ways, you're probably spending too much time creating it. This isn't to say that you shouldn't be constantly creating, but everything you've created can be repurposed in interesting ways. Quotes from blog posts or lyric snippets can be tweeted out to your Twitter followers. Old blog posts can be reconfigured and re-titled. Controversial posts could be revisited and re-examined. Podcasts can be turned into videos. Videos can be turned into podcast segments or press releases. Always look for ways to rework existing projects to help you create more traction. This is also a great way to gain attention for things that didn't go over that well the first time around. If a content piece didn't strike a note with your audience when you first posted it, it may resonate the second time with a new title.

- **Add value:** I've probably flogged this point to death already, but it bears repeating. The best way to get more social followers is to give people a reason to follow you. Whatever you win people *with* is what you win people *to*. If you win people with spam and false claims, they're going to resent you later. If you win people with value, the exchange of value between you and your followers will be ongoing. Answer questions and try to be helpful. Don't get too carried away with self-interests.

- **Use compelling call to actions:** "check us out" is *not* a compelling call to action. You know that already. Developing call to actions around giveaways is quite possibly the best way to engage. For example, 'Take our survey and get a free download code!' You can certainly frame the offer in more persuasive terms. The point isn't to avoid call to actions; I am not saying that at all. The point is to create messages that people will *want* to respond to.

- **Stay consistent:** consistency lends to your credibility. It shows that you're always up to something. It shows that you are persistent and worthy of following. It shows that you care about the people who follow you. Social media doesn't have to take a lot of time. What matters is that you don't just tell people to buy your stuff.

- **Learn about your audience:** it's one thing to attract followers - it's quite another to develop a lasting relationship with them. Though social media based friendships aren't always deep, it's the best tool you have to communicate with people that spend a lot of their time connected to their favourite networks. Moreover, your messages can still be delivered in a personal tone. If people are following you, it's because they want to know more about you. When you can address community members by name and chat with them about a topic that they are interested in, you know that you've taken adequate measures to build relationships with the people that care about you and what you do.

- **Create useful content:** content creation ensures a steady flow of new items to share with your social followers. Moreover, it's still one of the best ways to pique the interest of your audience. A blog post with a compelling title is going to draw people in to a conversation. At the very least, it will get people to your website. If your website is set up correctly, you may sell an album or gain a mailing list subscriber in the process.

- **Make your content shareable:** people love to share things that support their viewpoint of the world. If you know who your fans are and what subjects they're interested in, you can create content that they are more likely to share. There are also general topics that most, if not all people like to learn about (money, relationships, travel, etc.). If you can present your content in an interesting way, some of these interests might be worth talking about as well.

- **Pay attention to your branding:** make sure it is consistent across your various profiles and pages. If your Facebook page features a professionally designed logo, your Twitter page should not have an image that looks like it was developed by your teenage nephew. Moreover, the look and feel of your branding from one network to another should be fairly coherent. You don't have to use exactly the same images, but you should make sure that your logo is intact.

- **Learn from others:** are there specific social media personalities (like George Takei or Guy Kawasaki) that you love to follow? Do you have any friends that get hundreds of 'likes' on their status updates? Pay attention to these people, and figure out what they're doing right. You don't have to do what they're doing, but you can imitate their strategies and experience similar results.

>> Tools & Tips

To access these and other resources, go to:
http://dawcast.com/the-new-music-industry-resource-list/

> ➢ **Maximise the Power of Your Brain - Tony**

Buzan MIND MAPPING: if you aren't sure how to go about creating a mind map, here's a video detailing the benefits of mind mapping. Creator Tony Buzan himself explains.

➢ **How to Run a Successful Time-Based Crowdfunding Campaign:** again, there is a lot of information out there about how to run a successful crowdfunding campaign. I happen to like what the good people at HubSpot are doing, so I decided to feature this particular article.

Conclusion

I know that I've talked about a lot of different social media platforms, but trust me when I say that there are many more I could have touched on. In short, I wouldn't want to cause overwhelm and have you think that you have to *be everywhere*. That is a tactic that has worked well for some, but it takes a lot of determination, consistency, and most of all, time.

Setting up a social media profile and properly branding it will always take an upfront investment of time. Therefore, it might be wise to tackle one or two tools at a time and get a feel for them. Although some of them have familiar elements, each interface is a little different, and your customization options also vary based on the platform.

I would prepare all the images you need for your branding and put them in a convenient folder on your desktop labelled 'Social Images'. There's a cheat sheet for the various sizes of images you will need to create for the disparate social platforms (to access this resource, go to: **http://dawcast.com/the-new-music-industry-resource-list/**). As inconvenient as it may seem, every social network requires different profile and cover art image sizes. You just have to work with it.

Facebook seems like a no-brainer right now, and should probably be a part of *most* bands' marketing efforts. I can't really think of any band that shouldn't be on Facebook, but there are always exceptions. Moreover, I have always felt that one's personal website should be priority over social media. Social media is fine and dandy, but you need a central hub from which it flows (as Kevin Pauls noted in episode 26 of the podcast), and in general, it just makes you look more professional.

If you're already up and running, that's great. Commit to engaging regularly and actually think about your goals and what you want to accomplish through your interactions. Put some thought and planning behind your posts. Come up with themes if you think that might help you. For example: post pictures on Mondays, post videos on Wednesdays, and post concert write-ups on Fridays. Come up with your own scheme. Take the time to review your stats too.

What I Like

➤ **Google+:** frankly, Google+ is an amazing social platform. It has the best functionality of any network that's out there, and it's one of the best places for content creators to be. Having said that, I don't think it's going to replace Facebook, and it's doubtful that it ever will. The platform with the best feature-set does not always win. If I've piqued your interest, I would recommend spending some time getting to know how Google+ works.

➤ **Buffer:** while I still love HootSuite, I have found that the message scheduling process is much quicker on Buffer. To be able to queue up an unlimited number of posts (you can only schedule so many with the free version), you have to upgrade to the paid version. However, it is worth the price of admission, especially if you have a lot of content pieces you want to share with your audience.

What I Don't Like

➤ **It can be a time waster:** if you don't regulate and monitor the amount of time you spend on social networks, you could end up wasting a lot of time that could have gone towards more productive activities. If you find that you are often distracted, you may have to set some boundaries for yourself. You have to keep your priorities in order.

➤ **Setup:** after a while, you get to the point where you can set up new profiles on the various platforms very quickly. However, it does take some practice to be able to get to that point. Disparate platforms require different image sizes, and while some support more text, some require less. Some will allow you to enter more information, and others don't let you customize at all. You have to work with it the best you can.

Action Steps

➤ **Create a plan:** define your goals, create short-term, mid-term and long-term campaigns, and build your social presence around your projects; past, present and future. Bring it all together in a cohesive way.

➤ **Set up your profiles:** select which social networks you intend to use, and set up all of your pages and profiles. While it can be useful to set up personal accounts, make sure to create fan or business pages for your band if the platform allows you to do so.

➤ **Connect your blog, your email service, and your social networks:** in some cases you may want to cross-post from one social network to another. You will likely want your blog content pushed to the various social outlets the moment you publish something new. You may want to connect your social accounts to your email service so that you can make your newsletters available to your social followers. There are a lot of different ways to connect each of the platforms, and none of them are wrong or right; it mostly depends on what you want to accomplish.

➢ **Engage frequently:** keep at it! Engaging on social media can sometimes feel like shouting into an empty void, and a lot of the time, *it is*. Having said that, you will connect with more people in time. You will get more 'likes' and followers. Your posts will get shared. You just have to keep doing it even when it looks like nothing is happening.

➢ **Stay consistent:** the ROI (return on investment) of social media marketing is pretty disheartening at first. There's a lot of upfront work, be it planning or setting up your pages and profiles. However, the long-term benefits that can be gained from staying steady are well-documented. It just comes back to your goals and your mindset. Use social media for *socializing*, and you can't go wrong. Use it as a marketing outlet, and you may become frustrated.

15. YouTube & Video Marketing

 Distribution has really changed. You can make a record with a laptop in the morning and have it up on YouTube in the afternoon and be a star overnight. The talent on YouTube is incredible, and it can spread like wildfire. The downside is that it's very hard to convince the younger generation that they should pay for music. - Bonnie Raitt

YouTube is ubiquitous. It is quite easily the most popular video sharing site on the internet. It's also the second most popular search engine, just behind Google. Incidentally, it is also owned by Google.

While YouTube may not be the only video site you could create a presence on these days (and I am going to touch on other video sites in this chapter), it's a bit of a no-brainer. If you had to choose one video sharing site to be on, YouTube would be it. However, much like anything else in music, unless you put effort into marketing, you aren't likely to see a huge return on your activity.

Artists like Jack Conte from Pomplamoose have pointed out that YouTube used to be a great place to be, but now Kickstarter is where artists should be investing their time. I have heard artists say that podcasting is dead (it may have experienced a bit of a lull, but it's definitely not dead; it's actually going through a resurgence right now). Some people make it sound like jumping on the latest social trend is the best artists can hope for. Not only do I disagree, I don't believe any one tool has the ability to make you successful.

More to the point, I don't buy in to the idea of saturation to begin with. Some artists are always looking for the "next big thing" and I think that's fine, but no matter what tool you use, it's just a tool. It doesn't have any inherent ability to make you any greater or any lesser than you already are. You're going to have to get your music out into the world, and you're going to have to work at it no matter what method you choose. Quite simply, some vehicles will suit you better than others.

Moreover, **technological determinism** is a bit of a slippery slope. It's the idea that technology is the primary driver of the music industry. While it may play a significant part in the execution of marketing and distribution, there are a lot of other components that it simply cannot touch. *Never forget that.*

For example, technology can't really write a great song or great lyrics for you. Even if it could, what would people think of that? Technology can't mix and master your song. It can automate the process somewhat, but a great mix is still going to come from an experienced engineer with a good set of ears.

Technology can't duplicate the soul and emotion of a human musical performance.

In short, don't be too quick to buy into the idea that one website or app can make or break your career. It's simply not true.

Introduction to YouTube & Video Marketing

If you are 35 or younger, YouTube is already part of your day-to-day consciousness. You use it to listen to music, watch your favourite TV show, check out concerts, and find other interesting content to watch in your spare time. If that describes you, no matter what age you may be, you already know how people use YouTube to search for videos they want to watch. In other words, **if you want to know what people are searching for, you have but to become an observer of your own searching habits**.

A lot of musicians don't even give their videos a proper title and are surprised by the fact that people never find or watch their videos. Great content does not negate the need to practice basic SEO tactics. Your videos should have descriptive titles and detailed descriptions. If you *really* want people to find your videos, you can't leave anything to chance.

You also need to be aware that there are other video sharing sites you can distribute your content to besides just YouTube. Even if other artists aren't doing it, there are some advantages to being the only artist in a grocery market. That's just a figure of speech, but it can be taken literally as well.

That segues nicely into...

OneLoad

There's a handy tool called OneLoad that enables you to upload your videos to multiple popular video sites all at once (including YouTube). You will still need to set up accounts individually, but as you begin uploading more videos, the initial investment of time and effort will start to pay off, because you will be able to get your videos out to more sites quicker, with the same amount of effort.

Admittedly, the setup process on OneLoad can be a bit tricky. Some video sites require a two-to-three step approval process that you'll have to endure. I had some trouble with Veoh in particular, which asked me to check my email for a confirmation message which I never got, despite trying and re-trying. Then you have to plug in your login information or API keys into OneLoad, which can also take a bit of time.

Nevertheless, your efforts will bear fruit if you are willing to get through the setup process.

Additionally, there are a few key ingredients you'll want to be prepared with for every video:

1) **A title**: your video's title should contain your main keywords and key phrases. Many artists are not using titles to their advantage. Make sure to take some time to craft a relevant one.

2) **A short description**: all video sites have a limit to the number of characters that you can use in the description field. Unfortunately, they're all over the place, and some only allow shorter descriptions. Since YouTube allows for quite a bit of space, it may be profitable to go into your YouTube account to re-optimize your videos later once your videos have been uploaded across all of the sites. Also, it's definitely a good idea to put a link to your website (full URL including http://) in your video descriptions; preferably on the first line.

3) **Tags/keywords**: keep in mind that unlike blog posts, audio and video files can't be read by search engines. What this amounts to is that your title, description and tags or keywords are the only elements search engines can use to categorize and catalogue your content. While you don't have to be prepared with lots of pertinent words and phrases, make sure to use several relevant, quality keywords. Another good trick is to find what tags and keywords are being used on other popular videos, and adding those to your own.

OneLoad is a "secret weapon" that is often used by marketers, but I don't know too many musicians that are using it. It won't necessarily fast-track your career to success, but if there's an edge to be gained, it's worth looking into.

The Importance of Your Video's Title

I have seen many artists fail to take advantage of their video titles to maximum effect. I believe that a little bit of tweaking would drive more traffic and lead to more subscribers for many of these artists. Don't let laziness get in the way of creating attention for your videos.

First of all, you should try to avoid generic, vague or absurdly keyword heavy titles. The point is not to stuff your title full of keywords; the point is to provide enough keywords that your videos are more discoverable in search results. Consider what keywords people might be searching for, or do a search yourself and see what similar videos are titled.

For example, if you have a video of your band doing an acoustic cover, take full advantage of every relevant keyword, which would include your band's name, the title of the song, the other band's name, and the words 'acoustic' and 'cover'. Make sure to organize the title in a meaningful (and readable) way, but if you're not at least using these items in your video title, you're definitely missing opportunities.

Here are a few additional tips for crafting an engaging title:

- **Create great content that your audience is looking for:** a great title all begins with great video content. When you know what your audience is searching for, it's easier to create content that they will be attracted to.

- **Learn the art of copywriting:** aren't you glad I dedicated an entire chapter to this subject now?

- **Use numbers:** top 10 lists (like 'Top 10 Ways to Market Your Music Online') work just as well for videos as they do for articles and blog posts. In fact, the number does not have to be 10. It can be just about any number. Numbers can also be used in other ways. For example, 'How to Create a Viral Video in 60 days'.

- **Use an engaging video thumbnail:** include the title of your video (in text) in the thumbnail, and use your picture too! A video thumbnail is a bit like a blog post headline. It has the ability to capture the attention of people upfront without them knowing exactly what your video is about.

> ## >> Tools & Tips
>
> To access these and other resources, go to: **http://dawcast.com/the-new-music-industry-resource-list/**
>
> > ➤ **How to Write a Title for your Next YouTube Video:** this video elaborates on the topic of engaging video titles.

How to Optimize Your Video's Description

Perhaps the greatest sin you could commit with YouTube uploads is to fail to utilize the description field. YouTube doesn't really give you any other space to provide textual content (besides the titles and tags), remember? Not only will your viewers thank you for providing additional information, you'll be able to do a lot of wonderful things like:

- Drive traffic to your website by including your website's URL in the first line of the description (complete with http://).

- Drive sales to your music by including links to iTunes, Bandcamp, Amazon, etc.

- Drive traffic to other relevant content; blog posts, articles, podcast episodes, and other videos if applicable.

- Add value to others by linking to their channels or content if they contributed in any way (if applicable).

- Build your mailing list by letting your viewers know about your newsletter and linking to it.

So don't forget to write up a summary, break up the text to make it readable, and include relevant keywords and key phrases too.

Here's how to craft great descriptions for your videos:

- **Include a link to your website in the first line of the video:** I already gave you this tip, but it just so happens that it helps with creating an effective description as well.

- **Make it informational:** descriptions that provided the viewer with valuable information tended to do better in search results compared to videos that only contained navigational (links) or transactional (i.e. "buy here") descriptions. Long, keyword-rich descriptions are not only allowed, search engines favour them! Use terms like 'how to', 'learn', 'what is', 'what are', and 'history of' in your description.

- **Add tags:** use relevant keywords.

- **Choose a category:** find one that fits the content of your video.

>> **Tools & Tips**

To access these and other resources, go to: **http://dawcast.com/the-new-music-industry-resource-list/**

> ➤ **Learn How to Write Effective YouTube Descriptions that Search Engines Love:** if you'd like to learn more about the subject of video descriptions, consider perusing this resource.

Populate Your Profile

One of the advantages of having a social profile is that you can populate it with your own picture, cover art, relevant links to your website or other social profiles, among other items. I would definitely recommend taking some time to flesh it all out on your YouTube channel so that your viewers can get a sense of who you are, find out where they can buy your music, and where they can access more information about you. In short, make the effort to **brand your channel**.

YouTube continues to tweak and modify user options. Any information that I provide here could be outdated in a short amount of time. However, I will do my best to cover the basics:

- **Channel name:** YouTube will allow you to pick a name for your channel. By default, it will ask you if you want to use your Google+ account. I *would* recommend setting up your Google+ profile regardless of whether you intend to connect it with your YouTube account or not. However, YouTube does provide you with another option. You can click on "To use a business name, click here." to christen your channel with a company name. A single user *can* create multiple channels, so even if you screw up the first time, you can always try again.

- **Channel icon:** add a profile picture. If you are a solo artist, use a picture of yourself. If you're in a band, use a band photo. If you're going to use a band photo, make sure to use an image where you're all standing close together, so even at smaller sizes (your channel icon won't appear very big on your channel page), people can see who's who.

- **Channel art:** Google recommends using a 2560 x 1440 px image for your channel art. *Please* make note: **this**

can be a powerful promotional tool if used correctly. You can use this space to display call to actions, promote tour dates, or even market your latest single. A picture of an iceberg might look cool, but it's not going to do anything for you. A properly configured channel art image can increase traffic to your website, build your mailing list, or help you to sell more albums.

- **Channel description:** you haven't forgotten what I said about descriptions in the previous section, have you? If YouTube provides you with the chance to enter text, then *do it*! Yes, use your band name. Yes, use your album names. Yes, use keywords. However, don't forget copywriting 101. If you can engage, you will get more people looking at your channel.

- **Links:** you can provide links to your website and your social accounts that will overlap your channel art. Make sure to do this so that your fans can find you elsewhere on the web.

- **Feature other channels:** YouTube lets you link to other channels and 'feature' them from your channel page. The best way to use this feature is to develop relationships with other community members and cross-promote them. Even if not for that, you can give a little link love to channels and personalities you personally enjoy.

- **Channel keywords:** yes, YouTube even allows you to enter relevant keywords for your channel. Take advantage of this feature.

Interact

If you want to promote your channel on YouTube, take some time to interact with other community members. Not all of your efforts will generate results (or immediate results), but commenting on other videos, liking some, adding some to your favourites or playlists, and subscribing to other channels are but a few ways you can make your presence known on YouTube.

Don't put too much emphasis on this activity, as watching dozens of videos can be a bit of a time-sink. However, if you put a little bit of effort towards developing relationships with other YouTubers in this way, it can definitely complement your other marketing endeavours.

Here are some basic do's and don'ts for interacting.

Do:

- **Create great content**. Interesting, engaging and entertaining videos will win over more people than anything else you can do on YouTube.

- **Add value:** when you create value for others, it will always come back to you in some way.

- **Offer giveaways:** people love free stuff. Since you will probably have some cracked CDs, tattered T-shirts or frayed wristbands, you can always give them away. Subpar quality is okay when it's free.

- **Mention active followers:** if any of your followers or subscribers regularly make comments on your videos, make sure to mention them in your video(s).

- **Collaborate:** I will be talking more about collaborating later on in this chapter, but it is definitely a good way to orchestrate some great marketing and cross-promotion opportunities.

- **Spread the word:** word-of-mouth marketing is the most powerful form of promotion. If your video content is noteworthy, it will spread. When people are talking about your video at the coffee shop or on the street, that's how you know it's gone viral.

- **Watch, comment on, and like other videos:** get involved in the community.

- **Promote others:** I've always been one to promote things that I like, even if others told me that it was bad practice. After all, you never know when the favour might be returned. Even if it isn't reciprocated, I know that it will come back to me in another way.

Don't:

- **Solicit subscriptions:** people will subscribe to your channel if they like your content. It's your job to lead them to the water, but you can't make them drink. It's okay to ask in your videos. Just don't go all around YouTube asking for a favour.

- **Beg for views:** don't beg for anything in your career, period.

- **Comment for the sake of commenting:** YouTube comments are already notoriously bad. You don't need to add to the noise. If you're going to comment at all, leave a genuine, authentic comment. *That* will ultimately lead to more views for your channel.

- **Promise reciprocation:** for example, "I will like your video if you like mine". What *sounds* like a win-win is actually lose-lose, because you're wasting both your time *and* their time. Good videos will accumulate likes all on their own.

- **Spam:** no one likes spam. Not even a little bit.

Iterate

If something isn't working, don't be afraid to try new things. Learn from your mistakes and strive to improve.

While video is certainly a powerful platform, you have to keep in mind that there is a lot of clutter on YouTube. If you want to rise above the noise, you will have to help people find you. YouTube may seem like an equal playing field, but if you don't put the work in, no one will know that you even have a channel.

Jack Conte might very well be the king of iteration. Use him as your template. The reason Pomplamoose worked out so well is *because* he was willing to experiment and try different things.

Artists sometimes have a tendency to hold too tightly to their creations. If you want to find out whether or not something is going to work, then be prolific. Push out new content as fast as you can. If something doesn't work, you can still revise it. If it still doesn't work, you can try something else.

Taking action and making things happen is going to kill the suspense and anxiety of whether or not something is going to work out. If you're worried about how something is going to be received by your audience (or lack thereof), it's a clear indicator that you're leaving too much time between projects.

Stay Consistent

Creating consistency on YouTube can be very helpful in developing a viewership. However, in case you didn't know, creating and editing a video can be a fair amount of work. If you think you can create a new video every day, I wouldn't stop you. However, I would recommend no more than one per week and no less than one per month. First, create anticipation with your viewers. Then, fulfill that anticipation at the expected time.

If I'm not mistaken, like blog posts, you can schedule when you want your videos to go live as well. Use this feature to your advantage.

For example, begin by creating four videos. Then, when they're ready, schedule them out over the course of the subsequent four weeks. That way, you will have built up a bit of a margin for yourself. You'll be able to spend those weeks producing new content.

Another time-efficient practice you should be aware of is **batch processing**. This is where you do a particular task all in one go. For example, if you are writing a blog post, instead of just writing one, you would spend an entire day writing to meet your weekly or monthly quota.

So, if you know that you want to produce four videos per month, you could schedule a day or two for filming. Then schedule a day for editing. Then schedule an hour or two for uploading and populating the info for your videos.

Staying focused on one task until its completion makes it easier to meet your goals and avoid overwhelm. Grouping similar duties together and doing them all at once can enhance your efficiency and productivity as well. Conversely, when you are trying to manage a variety of different activities over the course of a single day, you can easily feel tired and overwhelmed. People aren't really meant to multitask and jump around from one duty to another all day long. It can produce a lot of stress.

How to be Successful on YouTube

If you want to be big on YouTube, observe and mimic those who have had the type of success you desire. Your music is your music, but there are valuable lessons you can glean from people like Pomplamoose, Lindsey Stirling, Tiffany Alvord, OK Go and Igor Presnyakov. You don't have to *copy* what they're doing, but I would recommend becoming an observer of those who have created more success than you have. Maybe even collaborate with them if you can.

- **Craft an engaging channel name:** I'm not sure what the word "craft" means to you, but in this case, it means to mull over. I wouldn't necessarily say that your channel name is the *most* important thing, but oftentimes it is the first thing people see. If you aren't sure what to do, simply use your artist or band name. If you want to get creative, add 'TV' or 'Videos' or 'Show' at the end of your band name. No matter what you choose as your channel name, make sure to think it over before finalizing it.

- **Post often:** ideally, if you want to be successful on YouTube, you should be uploading new videos on a weekly basis. Like a TV show, a lot of people like to consume their favourite content at a set, weekly time (i.e. Thursday at 7:30 PM). Even if people don't watch your video the moment you put it out, if they have the expectation that you're going to be releasing a new video at the appointed time, they will visit your channel, more than likely, within a few days. For some content producers, creating new videos at weekly intervals is a full time job. Depending on the level of production you aspire to, this is not an exaggeration. If you don't have the bandwidth in your schedule to handle it, then start simple and produce less regularly, with the intention of ramping up your frequency and production down the line.

- **Create great content:** make videos that people want to watch. I know this may sound too simplistic to some of you, but if you are already in the habit of watching

YouTube videos on a daily basis, then you probably have a good idea of what *you* enjoy. Though you definitely shouldn't copy what others have done (that can have certain drawbacks), you *can* take the best elements of what you like and incorporate them into your videos. Additionally, make your videos exciting! Convey enthusiasm.

- **Set goals:** as with anything, it's important to set realistic goals that stretch you a little bit. At a most basic level, your goals should involve the regular development of new content and the sharing of your creations with your family, friends, fans and social followers. Without these activities, you may as well not have a YouTube channel. However, if your last video got 900 views, then make it your goal to get 1,000 views - in the same amount of time - with your next video. You may have to stretch yourself to make it happen, but if you're not growing, you're probably stagnating.

- **Develop original ideas:** in essence, there is nothing new under the sun. Nevertheless, once you have an idea that is interesting, it's important to stick to it. Yes, you can engage in a variety of different ways as a musician, but there is also something to be said for creating and meeting an expectation. If most of your videos are acoustic covers of your favourite tunes, then you should continue to provide similar content, and strive to improve a little bit every time.

- **Promote your content:** there are many free and paid avenues for promoting your videos. Social media is a no-brainer. Posting to your blog is a no-brainer. Sending out your videos to your email list is a no-brainer. However, this is where some artists stop. What you need to do is create a marketing checklist and procedure list for yourself. That way, you can refer to your marketing plan every time you upload a new video and follow the steps you've outlined for yourself and your team or band members. You can always add to it and subtract from it as necessary.

- **Engage with the community:** be yourself. I know that I often talk about online marketing and social media in business terms, but the reality is that these are supposed to be fun mediums. The more fun you have, the more you are going to attract people to your content. Hard workers don't always win, as much as I hate to admit it. I have watched others create blogs that grew very quickly – faster than any blog I've ever created - because they grasped the fact that social media is supposed to be fun. So, if you are interested in interacting with the YouTube community, then make it about others. Don't spam. Don't fake enthusiasm. Don't automate comments. Take a little bit of time – but not too much – to watch videos that others have created and make it a point to add value to them. Additionally, moderate the comments on your videos. Make it a point to mention the people who often leave comments on your videos.

- **Provide value first:** whether you are creating new videos or interacting with the community, remember to add value. Value will always be reciprocated, whether it comes back to you in the manner you expect it to or not. People love to learn. They love to be entertained. They love to laugh. They love to be important. Even if none of those components are fixtures in your videos, I'm sure you can find a way to pepper them in there. You can teach. You can entertain. You can make people laugh. You can make people feel important. Just remember to be authentic.

- **Use titles, tags, descriptions and categories to your advantage:** take the time to populate these fields every time you upload a new video. Great engaging titles will help your content to get clicked on more often. Carefully crafted descriptions can help your videos to be discovered in search, and they can add value to your viewers as well.

- **Add links to your website and social profiles:** it's a small thing, but a lot of artists forget to do this. There are going to be people that are interested in learning more about you after watching your videos. Why not provide them with the opportunity? Your website should definitely be your priority, but it's good to cultivate **social proof** as well. If you have a high number of 'likes', followers, and subscribers, it makes you look more trustworthy to new visitors. That may seem unfair, but it is nevertheless true. It's easy to stop a snowball, but it's difficult, if not impossible to stop an avalanche.

While we're on the subject, don't artificially inflate your numbers. You can pay for services that will get you extra followers, but it's not worth it. All you get is numbers; you won't generate more engagement, or - if you are monetizing your videos - more money.

- **Research keywords:** keyword research isn't exactly the easiest thing to do, no matter what medium you are creating content for. However, there are many benefits. You can identify what people are searching for. You can generate new ideas for content by targeting keywords you may not have considered using before. You can avoid creating content that people aren't likely to be searching for. Keyword ideas can be generated via YouTube's Keyword Tool.

- **Do your homework:** know your competition. Study the videos that are getting views, and observe the commonalities between them. What are they doing that you could be doing? Is there a way for you to create a video that's better than theirs? Is the market for your content saturated? Is there still room for you? Is it in a niche that's worth creating a video for? If you are willing to do your homework, you can make informed decisions instead of shooting in the dark and hoping that something will hit.

- **Advertise:** if you are confident that you have a great video that everyone should see, create a video ad for your music or your channel. Some people don't like ads and will never act on them. Some people will skip them as soon as they possibly can. However, advertising will still get you in front of more eyes. You can reach a lot of people. This is something you should experiment with when you have a budget for it. Don't overextend yourself.

Conclusion

Video is a fantastic medium, especially for music promotion.

If there's anything you should take away from this chapter, I hope that you've come to understand the value of *creating content strategically*.

Success on YouTube is talked about as if it's happenstance or miracle. *Be careful*. If you act haphazardly, you will also tend to reap random results. I'm not saying that a video *can't* come out of the woodworks and take people by surprise, but *I am* saying that you can be far more calculated than that.

You can check out the competition and learn from them. You can see what videos are doing well, and you can also find others that aren't. You can compare and contrast, and brainstorm ideas based on what you've seen. These things do not assure success, but it should get you consistently better results than others who are not doing any of the legwork.

The hard part is that musicians sometimes think of those who use trends and marketing tactics to their advantage as though they are doing something disreputable. However, I feel that you should know how to frame your content so that it gains more traction.

For example, which of these two headlines immediately grabs your attention?

Atomik Penguins releases new album!

Or…

Metal lovers bang their heads to Atomik Penguins' brand new record, featuring their most inspired work to date.

Even if the Atomik Penguins had a great album, no one would care if they used the former headline to promote their new music. It's just a fact. You can find facts in phonebooks; it doesn't make phonebooks any more interesting.

People care about stories, and as a band, you *always* have a story. It may take some digging to find it, you may even have to hire an expert to help you with it, but the extra work will be worth the effort.

What I Like

> **Creating videos:** though creating videos does tend to take a lot of work, it can also be a lot of fun. In 2009, I started uploading video game and movie related videos to one of my channels. I didn't necessarily create any content with lasting value, but the channel today has over 90 subscribers and 100,000 upload views. This is despite the fact that I didn't touch the channel for two years. You just never know what might connect with people, especially given some time.

- ➢ **Cross-promotion opportunities:** a YouTube channel does provide many cross-promotion opportunities, whether you are trying to get more exposure for your website or one of your products. You can direct people to your social media profiles, and you can spread your branding in your videos.

- ➢ **Personal connection:** videos can be more effective than blog posts simply because they allow you to connect with your audience on a personal level. Audio can also be quite effective in this regard, and a lot of people will invest more of their time into audio than video. However, video does add one more important component; the visual. Quick, engaging videos can help you to create great connections with your viewers.

What I Don't Like

- ➢ **Editing video:** video can be a little fussy at times. Once you've captured your video, you may have to convert the file type. You may even have to find software to be able to do this in the first place. Then, once your video content is finally ready for editing, the software isn't exactly the easiest to figure out. If you don't have high expectations, then there won't be a lot of editing involved. However, if you want to insert pictures, mix footage, and keep the video engaging, it can be a lot more work. If you end up having to sync audio with video footage, I wish you Godspeed. In short, find an application and a process that works for you.

- ➤ **ROI:** quite honestly, video development can be labour-intensive. Don't get me wrong; the results can certainly be worth the effort. However, you don't have much control over what connects with people. At times, you may end up spending a lot of time on a video that no one cares about. Then, at other times, a video that you invested far less effort into grows in popularity. This is just the nature of art.

Action Steps

- ➤ **Decide whether or not you want to upload your content to numerous video sites:** OneLoad makes it easy for you to upload your content to multiple video sites. Is this something you want to do? Can you see yourself maintaining a presence on numerous video sharing communities? This is not an obligatory step. However, it is an amazing way to extend your potential reach. If this is something you know you want to do, it would be a good idea to start planning as soon as possible. Open accounts with each of the target sites. Get acquainted with them. Learn how to use each of them, as they all differ slightly.

- ➤ **Create a YouTube channel:** if you do nothing else, start a YouTube channel and add your profile information. Start uploading content as you are able. Video is a bit of a no-brainer for musicians, as music can be a highly visual medium.

- ➤ **Brand your YouTube channel:** brand your channel by adding an icon, channel art, and a compelling description. *Perception matters*. If your channel looks like it was put together by a 12-year-old, then you aren't going to stand out or look professional. If your channel art makes it look as though thousands of people *should* be (and are) following you, it will lend credibility to your name.

➢ **Create and upload engaging content on a regular basis:** without content, you have nothing. If you want to be successful on YouTube, at some point, you're going to have to commit to producing regular, entertaining videos for your audience. Some YouTube personalities and musicians make their living exclusively from YouTube. If that's not your goal, then you can get by on fewer videos. However, if you consider video marketing an important part of your online strategy, it's going to take some planning.

16. Conclusion

Many authors, bloggers and experts in the industry tend to present their opinions in an idealistic manner.

"Wouldn't it be nice if it worked this way?"

"If you did this, you should get these results."

At the end of the day, much of it is theory and speculation, **even my own prose**. *Unless you understand the mindset and approach behind the method, it's hard to duplicate what others have done.*

Moreover, as Andrew Dubber noted in his e-book, *The 20 Things You Must Know About Music Online*, a lot of what you hear in the media today is hype. Overnight success doesn't *just happen* to the overwhelming majority, no matter what the headlines say. News is often dramatized; it sells better that way. Journalists are looking for a good story, not a bland, everyday everyman editorial. Journalists - much like musicians - have to appeal to the heart, not the mind. They aren't necessarily malicious, but I think it's important to remember that they have a job to do too.

Lately, I've been hearing an awful lot about Amanda Palmer (partly because of her massively successful crowdfunding campaign) and DIY success Macklemore & Ryan Lewis. I don't doubt that either of them are hard workers. I don't deny that they have a certain appeal. I wouldn't discredit them from their accomplishments. However, the media's love affair has a lot to do with the fact that *their experiences make for a good story*, and that's why they keep showing up in the headlines. Their stories can be related dramatically. They can also be embellished if necessary.

I think Dubber's assertion - "don't believe the hype" - couldn't be truer today. As an aspiring musician, you could get discouraged looking at the news captions. You could get disheartened that you're not getting recognized in the same way other artists are. It doesn't always come back to skill or talent. It often relies to a marketable story.

The Cementing of a New Model

My gut feeling is that the framework of the new industry is solidifying. A lot of people are still in "waiting mode", but what we see now *is* the future of music. Allow me to explain.

CD sales are still thriving in certain sectors, but if you were to look at the statistics, you would see that it's definitely declining. Vinyl sales are up, but who knows how that's going to pan out? I'm not saying that it will die, and it is a decent market, but it's definitely not enough to warrant another format shift (or reversion). Digital sales are doing okay, but they haven't replaced CD sales and show no signs of doing so. It may seem depressing, but I don't feel that there will be a physical replacement for the Compact Disc. The sooner you can embrace that reality, the sooner you can get a handle on where things are going.

I'm not here to discourage you. Ultimately, I want you to recognize that even in this climate, in the midst of this seemingly tumultuous time, there are people with enough sense, perspective and old-fashioned roll-up-your-sleeves work ethic that are making their musical dreams a reality. There are musicians who are growing their businesses, making a living, even *making a killing* in today's arena.

Just look at Tom Hess, Pomplamoose, David Nevue, or Jonathan Coulton. What these artists have in common is that they are continually iterating and trying different things. Diversification is really the name of the game right now, and you have to be willing to create multiple income streams to make a living in music today.

There is no cure-all, at least not that I'm aware of. Be willing to go out and fail; multiple times if necessary. Success doesn't necessarily look neat, organized, or pretty.

17. Acknowledgements

James Moore for writing the foreword and for pulling the best out of me. This project would not be what it is without your feedback and suggestions.

Maveen Kaura and **Adam Meachem** for editing this book and giving me feedback on how to improve it.

Corey Koehler, **James Moore**, **CD Baby**, **Keith A. Link**, **Sean Harley [Tucker]**, **Matthew Jensen**, and **Music Centre Canada** for providing cross-promotion opportunities.

James Moore, **Maveen Kaura**, **Dayne Shuda**, **Sean Harley [Tucker]**, **Tom Jeffries**, **Jonathan Ferguson**, **Adam Meachem**, **Corey Koehler**, and **Keith A. Link** for your advance praise and support.

Andrew Dubber, **David Hooper**, **Derek Sivers**, **David Nevue**, and **Bob Baker** for continually inspiring my work and message.

Anna Mae Alexander, **Stefan Hills**, **Gabriel Binette**, **Jonathan Ferguson**, **Sharon Langendoen**, **Jennifer Wiebe**, **Fern Phillips** and **Bryan Phillips** for supporting me.

Riley Armstrong, **JJ Soriano**, **Tommy Tallarico**, **Pete Lesperance**, **Derek Sivers**, **Lucas Chaisson**, **Adam Burwash**, **Patrick Zelinski**, **Shawn David Evans**, **Karl Abrahamson**, **Chris Naish**, **Keith Skrastins**, **Daniel Guy Martin**, **Tatenda Mambo**, **Jonathan Ferguson**, **Derrick Mitchell**, **Nathaniel Krieger**, **Anna Mae Alexander**, **Mark David Stewart**, **Benjamin Perrin**, **Jadesong**, **Kevin Pauls**, **Chase Padgett**,

Steve Taylor, Dave Chick, David Hooper, Todd Henry, Kevin Breuner, Larnell Lewis, Christopher Knab, Lewis David Levin, Mike Doerksen, Sean Harley [Tucker], Maria Doll, The Philantropist, Allistair Elliott, Maveen Kaura, Corey Koehler, and Dave Cool for participating in interviews and/or the podcast.

Kira Dineen, Maveen Kaura and Tom Jeffries for contributing articles to the blog.

18. About The Author

David Andrew Wiebe started taking interest in music at the age of 14, and spent much of his free time in both Jr. High and High School writing lyrics.

At age 15, he performed a rap in front of an audience for the first time and learned the thrill of performance. When he was 17, he started learning the guitar, and quickly became known for his fast developing ability.

In ensuing years, he would go on to start a home studio, play in a variety of different bands, and embark on a teaching career. He would also work as a freelance graphic and web designer, online marketer and blogger on the side.

In 2005, his band, Lightly Toasted Touché released their first EP, *A Tale of the Coming Together and Murder of My Heart in the Golden State*. In 2006, Wiebe released his first solo album entitled *Shipwrecked... My Sentiments*, which showed considerable promise. He strongly believes he is capable of much more today.

With Angels Breaking Silence, he played guitar on "Boxes", a track that appeared on the *Unified by Grace Midwest Rock Volume No. 0002* compilation. In 2011, he appeared on The Active Light's "The Dark Has Had Its Day" as a guest guitarist. In 2012, he played lead guitar and mandolin on Jonathan Ferguson's *Sweeter After Difficulties*. He also co-produced, mixed, mastered and engineered Andrew Riches' solo debut album, *12 String Monster* the same year.

Wiebe founded The Music Entrepreneur in 2009, and continues to publish new insights into the music industry on a weekly basis.

19. Copyright Information & Disclaimer

For more music marketing tips, blog posts, podcasts, infographics, checklists, guides and other resources, visit: http://www.dawcast.com/

If you have any suggestions for future resources or if you'd like to send a letter of encouragement to David, email your comments and feedback to: comments@dawcast.com.

If you enjoyed this book, please consider mentioning it on your favourite social media sites using this hashtag:

#DAWTNMI

Disclaimer:

The views and opinions expressed within this book are those of the author, unless otherwise noted. *The New Music Industry: Adapting, Growing, and Thriving in The Information Age* is for entertainment and educational purposes only.

Third-party individuals, companies or websites mentioned in this book were referenced for illustration purposes only.

Notes

Notes